D1710809

Decorating with Color

Decorating with Color

CARLETON VARNEY

CREATIVE HOME LIBRARY
In Association with Better Homes and Gardens
Meredith Corporation

CREATIVE HOME LIBRARY

© 1972 by Meredith Corporation, Des Moines, Iowa

SBN 696-18600-4   Library of Congress Number 77-145625

2-24-75

Printed in the United States of America

Contents

About the Author

CARLETON VARNEY is president of the well-known interior decorating firm, Dorothy Draper and Company, Inc. Listed in *Who's Who in America*, Varney is decorator, painter, lecturer, and author of a nationally syndicated newspaper column, "Your Family Decorator," and several books, including *The Family Decorates A Home* and *You and Your Apartment*. Varney's interior decorating achievements range from hotels—such as the Greenbriar in White Sulphur Springs, West Virginia and the Sheraton-Waikiki, the world's largest convention hotel in Honolulu, Hawaii—to country clubs, banks, and private homes.

Preface

I believe that color is the most important decorating tool in the world. I also believe in bringing nature's outdoor colors into the home. When one attempts to improve on nature's colors, poor shades and tones result.

If I were to walk through a country garden and pick flowers for a bouquet, I would mix the daisies with the marigolds, the roses, the delphiniums, the purple asters, and of course, the green leaves. You can mix colors in a decorating scheme, too, for a beautiful look.

When I decided to write a book about color in decorating, I considered the subject very carefully. I was concerned about my approach, as were my editors. I did not want to write a pedantic book in school-room language, such as, "What is an analogous color scheme?" "Here are the earth colors," "These are the neutral colors," and "Those are the primary and secondary colors." There are many books written on the subject of color that show bars and graphs and give all kinds of formulas and principles. The books are good and of value; I do not mean to imply that they are not. Such books, however, rarely discuss color in terms of decorating. Rather they discuss color as a subject unto itself. As an interior designer I work with color all the time, but never out of context. The color I work with has a place, and that place is the home.

As I travel across the country on my lecture tour each year, I am always asked lots of questions. The great majority of these questions are about color schemes, followed by room arrangements and window treatments. Likewise, the readers of my newspaper column, "Your Family Decorator," write me all the time asking for help in solving their color problems. In this book, I am sharing some of the many questions I have been asked on the subject of color and my responses, or solutions, to the questions. In sketches I show settings for every room of the home, and in these settings I suggest many, many color schemes. Believe me, there is no end to the decorating color schemes which can be created.

Many wonderful people have participated in the writing of this book. First, I would thank the hundreds of people who have written me letters containing their questions about color. Without them the book would have been entirely different and not, I think, so enjoyable. Then I would like to give special thanks to Carol Breheny, Edward Evers, Ernest Fox,

Richard Hunnings, Elizabeth McAlpine, Tom Starling, Brenda Vennard, and always, my wife Suzanne and son Nicholas.

These friends and I have every hope that, through the pages of this book, you will enter the adventurous and delightful world of color, a magical world you will never want to leave.

—C.V.

New York City
1972

Introduction

If someone asked you, "What is your favorite color?" or "What is your favorite color scheme?" would you be able to answer? There are many people who know their favorite color—perhaps it is red, or blue, or green, or purple, or yellow, or pink, or brown. But many people simply do not. In my day-by-day contact with people seeking decorating advice, I use a few tests to determine color preference. One successful test is the "picture-color game." In my office I have a stack of hundreds of watercolors and prints. When I want to quiz a person about color, I quickly flash the pictures and prints, asking, "Do you like this print?" "Do you like this picture?" From the replies I build up a pile of "I-like" pictures, and a pile of "I-don't-like" pictures. After going through the complete stack of pictures, I examine the "I-likes" and generally find a pattern of color preference. The "I-like" pictures may all have reds and pinks in them or they may have combinations of blues and greens and yellows. "I-don't-like" pictures might have combinations of yellows and golds, or purples and oranges.

Another way to determine color preference is to examine your clothes closet. Do you buy more pink blouses than yellow blouses? If you do, you are partial to reds and pinks. If your yellow, beige, and gray blouses and skirts or dresses outnumber your red, pink, and mauve ensembles, you should definitely plan your decorating schemes around the soft colors you like, using vivid colors for accents only.

Linen closets can also give you a clue to your favorite colors. What color towels and sheets do you select? If you have a lot of light blue and white sheets and blankets and towels, you have an indication about your color choice. Plan a bedroom in blues and whites—with perhaps golds and/or greens for accents.

If you have lots of pinks, whites, and melon-colored sheets and towels, your bedroom decor might be fanciful and floral. Perhaps you would like curtains and bedspreads of a big flowered print—one that features orange and pink flowers with green leaves on a white background.

Try my "picture-color" game by going through an art gallery or museum or several books of art reproductions. Examine your closets and drawers—both yours and every member of your family's—to determine the favorite family colors. Then let these colors lead you into your own world of decorating with color!

Color it yellow. What a great color—this yellow! There is daffodil yellow, buttercup yellow, snapdragon yellow, lemon yellow, banana yellow, citrus grapefruit yellow . . . yes, there are thousands and thousands of yellows. I firmly believe that soft lemon yellow is as neutral a color as beige, white, or pearl gray.

Visualize your bedroom with lemon yellow carpeting. For those of you who like the sunny yellow and sky blue look, color your living room with sunshine nature colors. The yellow and red mixers might try a dining room styled with ruby red carpeting and soft lemon yellow walls. For the home with yellow bathroom tiles and white fixtures, what about using a lemon, olive green, and white striped covering on the walls?

Yellow is young and very much a Today decorating color!

Red is a sure-fire decorating color. If you were to name the brightest color around, I'm sure you'd say red. Red can bring lots of pizazz to any room in your home. There are all kinds of red colors, as the lipstick industry has proved. There is rose red, poppy red, fire engine red, wine red, brick red, cardinal red, strawberry red, to name a few.

Red-orange is one of my favorite colors in an emerald green, white, chocolate brown and cocoa decorating scheme. If you want to go star-spangled red in decorating the master bedroom, why not lay a bright flag red carpeting on the floor. Paint your walls a very light sky blue and your ceiling star white. For the blush of youth, try a red, pink, yellow and lime green scheme in a little girl's bedroom.

Red, black and white has always been a winning decorating color combination, and a library decorated with brilliant red lacquer painted walls says an immediate Wow! I like red felt walls, too. Whether you lacquer your walls red or cover them with felt, consider a black and white hound's-tooth rug for your floor.

Burgundy, the red wine color, is one of today's tones. Look at the fashion magazines and you are sure to see burgundy coats, suits, sweaters and hats. Burgundy has been a decorating color for years. Just look at those great Persian rugs with burgundy borders and centers of beige, pale blues, golds, pinks and just about any other color you can imagine. Not so long ago—about eight or ten years—Oriental rugs were being thrown out or given away, just for the asking. Not so today. Burgundy background Oriental rugs are in—in—in, with both traditional and con-

Introduction

temporary interiors. Why not take a color scheme from an Oriental rug and plan a dining room?

When you think red, you are picking a winning color. Red and brown and lime green is a winner. Red, white and blue is forever. Red, beige and purple is a new look with modern furnishings. Even red, orange, and yellow is a scheme for today.

Beginning with blue. Blue is one of the most favored of all decorating colors. When you think about blue, what comes to mind—sky blue, royal blue, navy blue, robin's-egg blue, electric blue, Wedgwood blue, Copenhagen blue, peacock blue, turquoise blue, cerulean blue, sea blue, delphinium blue or steel blue? I'm sure you can add lots of different blues to my list.

I am partial to light sky blue as a background color. I have always believed sky blue is the most neutral of all the colors. Sky blue works with everything. Nature used sky blue as a background color for a total universe, and against it set the greens of the grasses, the browns of the earth, and all the lovely country garden flower colors. How fresh and delightful is this sky blue!

For a modern dining room, what about a turquoise, fudge chocolate and bright white decorating scheme? The red, white and royal blue decorating scheme has recently become a rage in decorating; many of my friends and clients use the combination. For a great look in your living room, consider a combination of cerulean blue, emerald green, orange and white. I once decorated a bachelor apartment for myself in these colors.

The green light means "go," and the light is permanently flashing on Decorating Street, U.S.A. Never have I seen so many people selecting green for upholstery, carpeting, furnishings, and for just about everything else that goes into the home. Some time ago, while I was sailing off the New Jersey coast, I even saw a few olive green painted sailboats with olive green sails. The plastic laminate companies are making green-grained wood plastic laminates. The furniture houses are producing green-grained furnishings, many trimmed in color. Some are accented in red, others in yellow; and there are still others with white or with russet trim. Green-grained furniture can be most attractive in rooms that are brilliantly colored.

If you are a green thinker, you can come up with a host of different greens that are great on today's decorating scene: emerald green, kelly green, chartreuse green, sea green, pea green, avocado green and many many more. Apple green is the newest green to really hit!

The green and blue decorating combination of colors is a favorite of thousands. Why not coordinate a bedroom with these two color winners? And who said red and green was only for Christmas time? There are those I know who think of red with green in Christmasy terms only. Not me! I favor the combination, and my own library in the country is decorated accordingly. I love pine tree green and holly red in a decorating color scheme as much as I like the colors combined on a Christmas tree or a Christmas package.

Avocado green is a popular decorating color. May I suggest some color schemes that work with avocado and that can add a lot of spice to your home? For the living room carpeted in avocado, I suggest cantaloupe colored walls with a white ceiling and woodwork for the look of Now. A great bedroom could combine avocado, pale pink, shocking pink and white. Avocado and navy blue is a great color scheme if it is accented with lots of white and lettuce green. Avocado is not a color to mix only with beige, chocolate brown and rust.

There are lots and lots of people who like purple but never know quite how to use the color in decorating. I get many questions about the use of purple, lavender, violet, plum, lilac, and mulberry. Recently someone asked me to plan a living room around a purple rug. Another person asked me what color bedspreads and curtains to use in a room with lavender walls and beige carpet.

What colors *should* you use with a plum purple rug? How about pale light blue walls and spanking white trim? Then you can combine lavenders, violets, sky blues, grass greens, deep purples and tiger lily oranges in the fabrics. For a more subtle effect, I suggest lavender walls and beige carpet with fabrics of plum purple, lavender and emerald green. Lavenders and purples can be used with many colors. Consider lavender, sky blue and lemon yellow with some rich green accents. Lavender, brilliant red and pale melon can be a handsome color combination. So can lavender with black and white.

And yes, you can sweeten or spice up any room in your home by using one of today's biggest fashion tones—mulberry—a dark purple color. Never have I seen as many mulberry colored home furnishing items as have recently appeared on the market. There are mulberry, champagne and lettuce green fabric designs in bold scale and in small scale. There are mulberry lacquered coffee tables and dining room chairs.

Introduction

There are mulberry suede and mirrored cigarette boxes, and there are even mercury ginger-jar lamps with mulberry lamp shades.

I believe the popularity of mulberry has been created by the white modular furniture rage. As upholstery on a white fiberglass or plastic contour chair, what could be more effective than a bold geometric modern pattern of whites and lettuce greens on a practical mulberry-colored background? A word of caution: Mulberry is a strong color and must be used with lots of pale tones or with white. A total mulberry room would be dark and dreary.

In the pink! Pink is a fanciful color in the petal pink tone. It is also a dramatic color when you think of shocking pink. There are all kinds of pinks. There is baby pink for the little girl's room—that light and pastel shade. There are petunia pinks, peony pinks, rose pinks—all kinds of pinks can be used in the decoration of your home. Pink is not solely a feminine color—despite what some men think!

Visualize for a moment a pink, royal blue and lettuce green room. Pink is also a color to use with mandarin orange, sunny yellow and chocolate brown. Pale pink and emerald green is another of my favorite color schemes. Try it in your master bedroom.

For the look of springtime, perhaps in a little girl's room, what about a walnut, pale pink, shocking pink and lettuce green color scheme? For the kitchen in your home, try pink, royal blue and white.

Pink works with every color scheme and should not be relegated to the little girl's or baby's room. Be in the Now and Know! Try getting in the pink!

O is for orange. What comes to your mind when you think about orange? Do you see tiger lilies in the fields? A cozy fire? A ripe cantaloupe sitting on the breakfast table? A prairie sunset? An exquisite piece of coral jewelry? Or perhaps you see orange as a russet or coppery shade. There are many oranges, and all of them are being used in today's world of decorating.

The fall of the year brings the pumpkin into the limelight, and this particular shade—pumpkin orange—is a favorite with many because of its warm, but not too striking, or brilliant, glow. Why not consider a pumpkin, fudge brown, canary yellow, apple green and white decorating scheme for your master bedroom?

While there are those who prefer to use orange only with browns, beiges and avocados, some people can make orange come alive in a setting colored with brilliant tiger lily orange, fire engine red, shocking pink and royal blue.

For the friendly family kitchen, why not a mandarin orange, yellow and white color scheme? If the man of the house wants a quiet tweedy den with not too much color, I would recommend a chocolate brown, melon orange and beige tartan plaid.

Gold is one of the most popular decorating colors. There are many shades of gold, and you will assuredly be able to see the full spectrum at a local fabric house or paint store. Gold, avocado and orange is a very popular scheme; I have seen hundreds of rooms decorated with the combination. I do like to see a dash of shocking pink accenting the gold, avocado and orange rooms.

Mustard gold walls are a particular favorite of mine, provided all the woodwork and ceilings are painted clean white. For upholstery in a living room with mustard walls, choose a black and white floral print, or choose a print of gold, black and emerald green on a white background, or select a print of black, white and watermelon red. If you select an upholstery of black, white and watermelon, use watermelon rugs or carpeting. If you decide upon a gold, black and emerald green print, use emerald green for the carpeting.

The modernists have turned to shiny golds of a metallic finish for the young look. A metallic gold vinyl can enhance the walls of a room decorated with modern sofas and stainless steel or chromium-based furnishings.

The basic look of brown. When you think about brown, do you think of fertile soil, chocolate candy, tree bark, furs, coffee, tobacco or saddle leather? There are lots and lots of browns, and you assuredly have one of the many tones in your home, be it a tan naugahyde on a chair or a walnut stain on an end table. I love the look of brown, and I dare anyone to prove that it is impossible to use something in brown in any room of any home.

Brown means earth to me. It is solid, firm and weighty. When I think of brown, gravity comes to my mind. What home doesn't need a sense of gravity, of security. Homes also need brightness and air; therefore, I am against totally brown rooms.

Combine rich earth brown, emerald green and sunny yellow in your living room. Add a dash of paprika orange, and you've created a real look. Chocolate brown with sky blue and white is another decorating color winner. If you are a chocolate and red person, why not decorate a study or boy's room in these tones? Add champagne beige and white, and you have created an exciting room for your son.

The secret of working with brown is: Begin with brown, but don't end there! This rule of thumb is especially true of beige. I have seen a number of rooms across the country decorated with beige carpeting, beige walls, beige draperies, and different beige-toned upholsteries; they are lifeless and monotonous. Beige rooms can be successful only when furnishings have exquisite finishes, when lamps are filled with warm colors, and when wall hangings—paintings and tapestries—are alive with reds, greens, blues, yellows and other tones.

When decorating a room in your home, you can begin with warm beige . . . it is a beautiful soft tone . . . but don't end there unless you have other colors and an array of colorful paintings to bring cheer to your setting.

For the beige oriented, why not decorate a room with a champagne beige, melon, lettuce green and chocolate brown scheme? A champagne beige, fiery red and pale pink color scheme would be a hit in the master bedroom. For a young man's room or for a library a color scheme of beige, royal blue, emerald green and chocolate would be a winner. A beige bathroom can come to life with orange, yellow and emerald green.

Beige is a great decorating color, but should not be without some colorful company.

The great look of gray! Nobody likes gray days and I am no exception. I am all for sunshine in life. This doesn't mean, however, that I put down gray. It is a great and versatile decorating color. There are many grays: pearl gray, mouse gray, charcoal gray, flannel gray, silver gray.

If you want to give your living room a sunshine look with gray, try this scheme: paint your walls a soft flat pearl gray and your woodwork and ceiling a bright white. On the floor put a rich dark charcoal gray area rug bordered with daffodil yellow. Now visualize this background with fabrics of yellow, emerald green and orange. If you plan to decorate your dining room, what about using a scheme of flannel gray, brilliant tomato red and luscious lime green.

For a truly sophisticated decorating scheme in your den, try charcoal painted walls with white trim. Lots of pillows of animal skins would look good in this room, especially if it were furnished with modern white lacquered end tables and a stainless-steel-and-glass coffee table.

Gray can be combined with any color or colors you might wish.

I have always believed that every successfully decorated room features a touch of black—an ashtray, a lampshade, a coffee table, a vase, picture frames or the fringe on draw draperies. Black gives weight as well as drama to a setting!

When you are shopping for new furniture for your home, consider a black lacquered coffee table for that spot in front of your sofa. Or perhaps you will entertain the idea of a black console or commode for your foyer—one of those great-looking pieces with big Oriental hardware.

A friend of mine has a living room styled in black and white zebra print. That is what I call a knockout room. But black and white with a third color is even more impressive. Think of the number of rooms that are decorated in black, white and fire engine red. There are many rooms color coordinated in black, white and peacock blue—or in black, white and chocolate brown. One of my favorite schemes is black, white and emerald green, with just a dash of persimmon for accent. Visualize the foyer of your home with a black and white checked or striped vinyl floor.

I am a man who likes a touch of black in the bathroom. Picture a striking black, lemon yellow and white scheme in a bath with white, lemon, gray or black fixtures.

Black should never be viewed as too somber to be used in decorating. If you plan carefully, a touch of black can be one of your room's most exciting colors.

The wonder of white! I know a lot of people who dream of a white room. I only hope these people live where there is not much smog and dust. The white room is a dream room and, I admit, can be successful, but go lightly with white if you have children or pets.

If you are a white room enthusiast with contemporary taste, why not consider this plan? Use fabrics, paint, and rugs that are washable: enamel and lacquer for walls and furniture, fiberglass for casement curtains and nylon puff rugs. Use another color, in its palest tones, for interest, perhaps a pale green. Be sure to hang lots of colorful modern or traditional paintings with white frames on your walls.

A white and lemon yellow scheme, with just a dash of gold, is always successful in the bedroom. I also like kitchens planned in white provided there is a good color accent, perhaps a brilliant red ceiling. White with another color is sure decorating magic.

The Living Room

A living room is for living. If you are one of those people who want to create a perfect living room to be admired only, you are on the wrong decorating track. A living room to be admired is for a museum only; but a beautiful living room that can be lived in and enjoyed is—for me—the most rewarding and handsome setting.

Styles, furnishings, textures—there are so many aspects to consider in creating a living room decor. Surely the most basic consideration is the color scheme, but how does one go about selecting it? I suggest that you keep a scrapbook or folder filled with magazine pictures of rooms you like. When color-selecting and color-scheming time arrives, pull out your folder or scrapbook and take a good look at the color combinations you favor.

Visit an art museum with your family and this time really look at the colors in the paintings. Perhaps a walk through a modern art gallery will inspire your color scheme if your family appreciates today's colors. Or, you and your family might purchase a painting together and use the colors in the painting for your living room scheme. The strongest color in the painting can be your rug or carpeting. The lightest color in the painting can be your walls. The other colors can be used for upholsteries, curtains, pillow accents, flowers and accessories.

When planning a room's color scheme, consider your light source. If your room gets little light, pick sunny colors like soft lemon, warm sky blue, fawn beige or petal pink for background. Use bright fabrics to give your dark room real zest, and, above all, make sure you have enough lamps and lighting in your room. You might even install strip lighting— a warm white deluxe fluorescent tube—behind your drapery valance to give your window curtains a further glow.

If you have a very bright living room filled with lots of sunshine, you can choose bright garden colors or you can dramatize your setting with dark walls and bright colors in the furnishings. For instance, with chocolate brown lacquered walls and white trim you can use bright yellow carpeting and upholstery of yellow, cocoa, lettuce green and gold flowers on a chocolate brown background.

Ceiling height also determines color schemes for a room. If you have

1

a large high-ceiling living room and want it to appear lower and cozier, paint your ceilings a darker color than your walls. For example, you might paint your walls soft yellow and your ceiling a yellow gold. You might also consider pale blue walls with white trim and a Wedgwood blue ceiling. If your living room is small and has many doors, paint your doors, walls and ceiling the same color to unify space.

Remember that color determines the "mood" of a room. Do you want a bright, gay living room? Then have fun with lots of contrasting, sharp colors. Do you lean to the dramatic, exciting decor? Then plan a color scheme of two or three boldly contrasting colors; for example, black, white and red or blue, with accents of another color to highlight the drama. If a quiet, restful living room is your cup of tea, you may consider the neutral shades or a monochromatic color scheme. But quiet and restful does not mean drab and uninteresting; be sure to add some sharp or vivid colors in the accessories and accents to avoid a dull room.

Every living room has some wood furniture—tables, cabinets, chairs, etc.—and these are part of your color scheme, too. Certainly, wood paneling, if you have it, must be treated as one of the major colors in a room. Don't hesitate to mix woods or wood stains and finishes, just as you mix other colors in your living room.

No matter what "rules" are laid down by decorating authorities, you must make your own decisions. Your own taste must determine which "rules" you will adopt and—more important—which ones you will ignore. Any combination of colors is acceptable, if *you* like it. This is especially true today when people are using color combinations that were considered "impossible" just a few years ago. Patterns, prints, stripes are being used together most effectively in today's living rooms because we have learned how to tie them together with color.

Are you dissatisfied with your present living room? There are many ways to create a new one. Very few of us can discard everything and start from scratch. Changing a color scheme is the most effective way to bring about a transformation. Sometimes painting alone will do it; sometimes introducing new colors with slipcovers. You may have to find the one color that will unify an assortment of odd pieces, of hand-me-downs, of the room's present colors. Well-chosen colors for accent pieces or accessories can make an unbelievable change in a living room's appearance: a black lamp, a yellow vase, throw pillows in prints and solids. Make your living room live again—with color—so you and your family will love living in it.

Question: *The living room in our new apartment is quite small. In decorating, I want to keep it as light and "open" as possible. The walls and ceiling are white. How do I add color without losing the lightness? Is a white sofa too, too impractical?*

White adds space to a small living room. Color adds warmth.

A very small living room often should have lots of white to open it up. Upholster your sofa as well as a chair in a bright white, soft, washable glove vinyl. Use a pair of white lacquered cube end tables at the ends of your sofa. Then, for color lay a mandarin orange carpet on the floor and buy a rich lemon yellow lacquered coffee table. Bring further color to the setting with a modern painting, a colorful yellow lamp, and green plants.

Question: *I don't want the usual draperies or curtains at my wide living room windows, but I do want brightness. What can I do with them? I have a bright daffodil yellow carpet, a beige and white check print on the sofa, and white walls. What slipcovers would you recommend for two club chairs?*

Use the same print on fabric window shades and chairs to provide a living room with color.

Upholster your club chairs in a gay floral print of daffodil yellow, poppy red and mint green. Use the same print for Roman shades at your windows. Accent your sofa with mint green pillows, and cover the seats of two pull-up chairs with a snappy red naugahyde.

The Living Room

Question: *My living room is so conventional—it's dull! We are limited by existing sea green carpeting and draperies, though we can afford to change the draperies. The sofa is upholstered in sea green silk brocade, and two club-type chairs in a striped green-on-green silk. How can I make this outdated combination really swing? I am willing to make slipcovers.*

Shocking pink can be a good color for the living room.

I would suggest painting your walls a frosty white and your woodwork and trim the same. Hang shocking pink draperies edged in white under a white valance at your windows. Slipcover your sofa in a melon orange and shocking pink floral design on a white background. Use shocking pink throw pillows on your sofa and white porcelain end table lamps on end tables, if you have them. Leave your green chairs as they are. You might add an interesting pull-up chair to your setting; cover its seat in a shocking pink, melon orange and black needlepoint design.

Question: *My new three piece corner sofa is black vinyl and walnut. The carpet and draperies are a matching informal gold. The walls are white, and the woodwork walnut. I have a large bronze modern sculpture, a large white lamp on a black base and a large green plant in the room, besides several multicolored paintings. I've been thinking about buying two large side chairs in burnt orange or bronze crushed velvet. What do you think?*

Go Mexican in a modern living room.

Your room needs color—some fun accent colors. Instead of burnt orange or bronze crushed velvet on your new side chairs, I would use a bright lettuce green, emerald green and cantaloupe geometric print. The background of the print should be white. Mexican pillows in an array of different colors and designs on your sectional sofa would be great. Get a pillow or two in shocking pink, gold, emerald green and black stripes with tassel corners, a couple of Siamese tweed pillows, and a pillow or two in citrus green and sparkling orange. If wall space permits, hang a colorful woven Mexican modern tapestry above the sofa.

5

Question: *We are going to redecorate our living room now that the children are all in college. I plan to have slipcovers made for the sofa using a bright print of orange, yellow and brown. Our walls are white and the carpeting is very light beige. Above the sofa is a large oil painting of an autumn landscape. What color draperies shall I buy, and what can I do about a dark brown chair? Should we change the carpet, which is pretty worn anyway? How else can I brighten my living room?*

Brass end table lamps with white shades help a living room to glow.

Brass end table lamps with white shades would brighten your room, and so would a kelly green carpet and kelly green pillows on your sofa. I like slipcovers, and I recommend and use them often. Why not cover your brown chair in a bright orange and white stripe? Hang yellow draperies at your windows under a valance made of the same fabric you are using for the sofa slipcover.

Question: *I am doing some redecorating in our living room. These things will stay as they are: a champagne beige sofa, an occasional chair in orange, beige, and moss green and gold draperies. I want two new chairs, a coffee table and carpeting. What colors would you suggest for the chairs and carpeting? Lately I have noticed more ads for area rugs. Are they becoming popular again? Could I use an area rug in my 12-by-15-foot living room?*

Area rugs never go out of style—why not see an array of color under a glass-top coffee table?

If your living room has attractive floors, why not give yourself a change and have an area rug? I might suggest one in a patterned design of lemon yellow, melon orange, royal blue, avocado green and yellow beige. Perhaps the design might be Moroccan. Your new coffee table can be glass and steel. How great it would be to see the colors in the rug through your new glass table top. Your two new chairs could be a snappy stripe in lemon yellow, melon orange and royal blue on a yellow beige ground.

6

Question: *Our rather small living room has floor-to-ceiling windows. The rug is beige with a soft pink border. Our traditional English couch is a soft green and white stripe. What colors would you advise for the walls, new draperies, and a wing chair? Do I have to have white walls because the room is small?*

Draperies and walls in the same light color unify and enlarge a small living room.

Small rooms need light colors to make them seem larger than they really are. Why not paint your walls a pale pinky beige? The woodwork should be white semigloss enamel. To unify the room, tieback curtains can be pinky beige to match the walls, and the wing chair can be covered in the fabric to match the curtains. The draperies would be most effective trimmed with a beige and white braid. Accent the setting with Wedgwood blue accessories.

7

Question: *Our living room is rustic-looking, with earth brown vinyl flooring, white stucco walls, a fireplace and beamed ceiling. Furnishings include white draperies, two brown couches and two rocking chairs. Though comfortable, the room is drab-looking. How can I make it more alive? Would slipcovering the two couches do the trick?*

Orange and yellow added to brown infuses a living room with warmth.

Your room needs warmth and color. You should definitely slipcover your two couches in an orange and yellow geometric or floral print, perhaps with touches of red and gold. Accent the sofas with yellow or gold pillows. I would paint a large coffee table or end tables in pumpkin or mandarin orange lacquer.

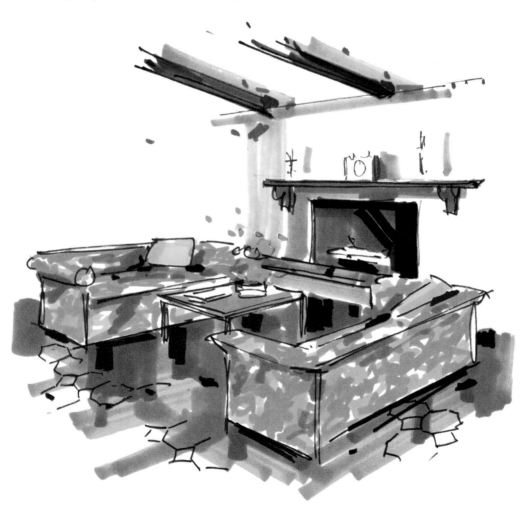

The Living Room

Question: *We have a mobile home. The walls in the living room are dark paneling. Our draperies are white, our carpeting is gold and our furniture is walnut. What color should we look for in a chair and couch to create a livelier room? Would a chain lamp be appropriate in this room?*

Brighten a mobile home's living room with more color than gold and white.

There are a growing number of mobile homes in the country, and mobile home owners always seem to be decorating. I would use a practical yellow, green and white printed fabric on your sofa, probably floral. Use a bright kelly green on the chair. Put yellow pillows on the sofa. By all means, hang a chain lamp in your living room—over an end table if you wish. Try a modern Tiffany-type fixture of white milk glass with brass fittings. The lamp might also be of lemon yellow glass with brass fittings and chain.

Question: *For my living room I have chosen a Mediterranean blue green sofa with an antique-white frame, a matching lounge chair, and two small antique-white coffee tables. My carpeting is a very pale gray. I would appreciate suggestions for draperies and a second chair. Also, what would you think of a mirrored wall opposite the room's picture window, which looks out onto the garden?*

A mirrored wall can reflect an outside vista and pick up the room's colors as well.

What about a sunshine yellow, melon and sea green print for draperies under a sunshine yellow valance? Your second chair can be covered in a thin yellow and white stripe. Pillows for your new blue green sofa can combine all your sunny colors—yellow, white and melon. Mirror the wall opposite your window, so that the mirror can reflect the out of doors as well as the colors of your new draperies and valances. On the mirrored wall, for a further touch of interest, try hanging some half-round white wicker planters filled with fresh green plantings.

9

Question: *A year ago I bought an Oriental rug and have tried to plan my living room around it. The rug's solid color is soft green. The figures on the edge and in the center are these colors: deep bright rose, pale pink, deep light blue, pale blue, gold and tan. My furniture is fruitwood. What colors would you suggest for my walls, draperies, sofa and club chair?*

The colors in an Oriental rug can offer an exciting decorating scheme for the rest of the room.

I would paint the walls a very pale champagne with white ceiling and woodwork. For draperies, I'd find a color to match the pale pink in your rug; line the draperies in white satin under pale pink simple shaped valances. Trim the draperies and valances with a pale blue, bright blue and white gimp. Cover your sofa in pale blue and your club chair in bright blue and pale blue stripes on a champagne beige background. For sofa pillows, I would use pale pink, shocking pink and sea green. To help your room achieve that special personality look, hang a variety of bright, colorful paintings featuring oranges, greens, delphinium blues, golds and sunshine yellows.

Question: *We live in a very old house. The living room wainscoting (from floor to halfway up the wall) has been painted over a number of times and is currently yellow. Our rug is green. We have heard wainscoting is "coming in" and should be preserved. Should we try to remove the old paint and utilize this old wood together with new plasterboard above, or should we panel over the entire room?*

In a living room with wainscoting, paper the walls above with a multi-color floral pattern.

By all means, keep the wainscoting. Paint it a pure white. You might have to patch it up first and then sand over it. Above the wainscoting—why not paper? Before you go to the expense of plasterboard, try filling the cracks with plaster of Paris and then sand over it to get a smooth finish. Now you are ready to paper. My choice of paper would be a tomato red, emerald green, and navy blue floral pattern on a lemon yellow background. This will look great with your green rug.

10

Question: *The upholstered pieces in our living room are bright yellow, white and sky blue. Our fireplace and wall are white, and so is the carpet. The room doesn't seem to "hang together." Would a new wall color be the solution? The room gets little natural light.*

For sunshine brightness and unity in a living room, let yellow predominate in a yellow, white and blue scheme.

Paint your living room walls buttercup yellow and your woodwork and ceiling snowy sparkling white. Keep the fireplace white, but use some Delft tiles around your fireplace opening. If you have an old wooden chest or cabinet, you might paint it clean blue and use it on the wall next to your fireplace.

11

Question: *I want to re-cover our modern living room furniture—an armless sofa and chair and a pair of square lounge chairs—in some modern colors. Our walls are white and our carpet is a pinky beige. What colors would be "different"?*

Magenta and pink is truly a contemporary color scheme.

Why not cover your sofa and armless chair in a pink and white tweed fabric and the two square chairs in bright magenta. Lacquer a coffee table with magenta, and use magenta throw pillows on the sofa. A modern abstract painting of stainless steel gray, pink and electric yellow would add lots of color to the sofa wall.

The Living Room

Question: *We are planning to redecorate our Early American living room by reupholstering a maple couch and hanging new draperies. Our walls are painted ivory, and our floor is wood tile. We have two oak chairs with avocado cushions. I would like to cheer up the room, but stick to a solid color for both couch and draperies. Should the couch and draperies match?*

Couch and drapery colors do not have to match.

Your couch and draperies need not match. Why not use a melon orange nylon tweed upholstery on your sofa and sunny yellow draperies at your windows? Pillow accents on your sofa can be melon and avocado. Though you like solid colors, your room definitely needs a print. How about a geometric or floral print in a shag area rug on your wood-tile floor? Melon, lemon and olive should be the colors in the rug.

Question: *We recently put imitation brick on our living room walls, so that our gray, turquoise and red color scheme needs to be changed. Please suggest colors for a new rug, couch and chair slipcovers, and draperies. I'm not too sure about what colors complement brick.*

Imitation brick can be used effectively with bright colors.

I love brick walls—imitation or real—and envy people who have them. Most bright colors go well with brick, including turquoise and red. But you seem to want a new look, which is fine. Since you have covered all your walls with brick, it sounds to me as though you would enjoy a country-style living room. I'd hang sunny yellow louvered shutters at the upper portion of the living room windows. The lower window portions can be treated with café curtains of a yellow, white, black and russet checkered fabric. Hang the curtains on a brass pole. On your floor use a yellow rug with a chocolate or russet border. Cover your couch in solid sunny yellow and your chairs in the same checkered fabric as the curtains. Throw pillows on the couch can be orange and chocolate brown. I'd also like to see a pillow or two of the checkered fabric.

Question: *Our living room carpet is a floral pattern, in green, rose and touches of blue and black on a beige background; the colors are very soft and blend well. Our walls are light green (paler than the carpet green). I would appreciate your suggestions for draperies, sofa and two club chairs.*

On solid-color draperies, use a border of a contrasting color.

Your carpet sounds lovely, and your living room sounds as though it has great potential. I would choose draperies in a soft champagne beige and trim them with a border of soft green to match the green in your floral rug. Sofa upholstery can be the same shade of green, with throw pillows of champagne beige and pale pink. You should consider a pink, beige and green stripe for the covering on your club chairs.

Question: *We have kelly green carpeting in our living room. The walls and draperies are white. In redoing our couch what colors should I look for? I was thinking of pale blue for the chairs and maybe a print for the couch.*

Floral patterns will never go out of style as long as gardens exist.

You are thinking in the right direction. A pale blue, lemon yellow and kelly green floral print on your couch would be mighty pretty. Cover your two chairs in a pale blue and white stripe. Your windows would sparkle if you would decorate them with curtains of the floral print under a white valance. The valance, for added distinctiveness, might be lined and trimmed in soft lemon yellow or white.

Question: *Please help me choose the right color paint for my living room walls, as well as the color for new draperies. I have a gold rug, a gold and olive couch, two olive chairs and a tangerine recliner.*

A gold and olive color scheme needs a pickup. Use a floral print of orange, yellow, and blue.

I recommend that you paint your living room walls sky blue with white semigloss enamel for the trim. Sky blue always provides a pleasant, cheerful background. For the windows, find a flowered print—perhaps lemon yellow, carrot orange and deep deep sky blue flowers with fern green leaves and walnut brown stems on a white background. If you have any fabric left over, why not slipcover one of your chairs with the same fabric? Put some lemon yellow, carrot orange and lettuce green throw pillows on your olive sofa.

Question: *I have a problem trying to decide what color to use on two chairs I want to purchase for my living room. I already have a three piece French provincial sectional sofa in ice white with a light blue design running through the fabric. My rug is blue, and I have blue and white draperies. I don't want any more blue if I can help it. Can you suggest a color for the chairs and also for the walls?*

Yellow relieves a too blue color scheme.

You certainly don't want to overdo any one color in a room, especially in a living room. Pale lemon walls with white woodwork would be my suggestion. I would find a yellow and white stripe for the new chairs. On a pull-up hassock and on sofa throw pillows, I'd use a bright watermelon color.

Question: *My fiancé and I have bought Spanish-styled furniture for the living room of our first home. The long couch is covered with red crushed velvet, and two high-back chairs are black crushed velvet. Do you have any suggestions about what color carpet and draperies we should use?*

Juicy lime green, torero red and black are great colors in Spanish-styled living rooms.

What about a rich, juicy lime green carpet? White heavy linen draperies, banded with a black border and lined in bright red would bring a bit of Spanish *olé* into your new living room. I'd suggest that the curtains be hung on black rings from a wrought-iron pole or a wood pole painted black. Your walls should definitely be white.

15

Question: *We are redecorating our living room, which is very traditional. What will stay "as is" are the carpet (a beige and green Chinese medallion design) and the sofa (beige-on-beige damask). A wing chair and a pull-up chair can be re-covered. Also we plan to buy new draperies. What colors do you suggest for everything including walls?*

With traditional living room furniture, try painting the walls an unusual but serene color, such as cantaloupe.

Soft melon walls with white trim would be my choice to go with your traditional furniture. Draperies can be beige trimmed with an interesting green and white braid. On a traditional wing chair, why not choose a gold and copper cut velvet upholstery? The seat of a pull-up chair can be bright gold.

Question: *My husband wants to cover the living room walls of the new house we are building with fruitwood paneling. I'm not sure the color scheme I've planned will look good with paneled walls. I would like black, green and yellow in the room. What do you think?*

Treat wood finish as one of the most important colors in a room.

Fruitwood walls would provide a great background for your color scheme. How about draperies and sofa fabric in green and black polka dots on a light gray background? One chair could be a bright canary yellow. Use the same yellow for throw pillows on your sofa. Carpeting can be green or dove gray. For accent colors about the room, use brilliant red and sky blue.

Question: *I have a dark blue couch and chair in my living room. The walls are now white. Could you suggest a different color for the walls? What color should I use for draperies and carpeting?*

Try hanging a multicolor drapery pattern in a silver frame for an effective spot of color.

I do not object to your white walls, but your room needs some print. What about hanging some bright yellow, emerald green and red print draperies at your windows under a yellow valance? Use bright red and yellow pillows on your couch, and install a vivid tomato red carpet on the floor. If you must change your wall color, I'd recommend sunny yellow with white woodwork and ceiling. For a final, conversation-piece touch, hang a width of your drapery fabric in a thin silver strip frame over your dark blue couch.

Question: *My husband and I are in the midst of redecorating our living room. Since the room is small, what colors should the walls, draperies and furniture be? The only item we have bought is a dark blue and green carpet. I realize a dark shade for carpeting in a small room tends to make it smaller, but we had to get a dark shade because of heavy traffic from our three children.*

Dark-colored carpeting is all right for a small living room if furniture is appropriately scaled and is covered with bright, colorful prints on light backgrounds.

There is nothing wrong with a dark carpet in a small area. If you are buying new furniture, as I assume you are, you should stay away from large-scale pieces. Furthermore, the furniture should be covered in bright, colorful prints on clean, light backgrounds to help create a more spacious look. I'd begin by painting your walls a pale lemon yellow and your trim white semigloss enamel. Your ceiling can be sky blue. Find a cotton paisley print of watermelon red, French blue, lettuce green and deep chocolate brown on a lemon yellow ground for your sofa and draperies. Cover two chairs in solid watermelon. End tables can be walnut; a living room breakfront can be white lacquer trimmed in blue; coffee table can be brass and glass.

18

The Living Room

Question: *My modern living room couch and lounge chair are charcoal gray, with frames painted black. I have stainless steel lamps and a white plastic cube coffee table. I have decided on a color scheme of charcoal gray, green and white, but don't know how to distribute these colors. Also, I realize the scheme needs an accent color or two. What would they be, and where would I put them? I don't want more in the way of furnishings; I like the uncluttered modern look.*

Pillows are a great way to bring new colors into a living room without making the room look "busy."

Why not start your color scheme with a modern area rug featuring bright green and a bit of yellow on a charcoal background? Paint your walls the bright green. Two accent colors which would look great in your living room are blue and yellow. Use them in throw pillows on your couch and you'll avoid a cluttered room. To add further brightness, you might lacquer your couch and chair frames white.

19

Question: *I know black and white can be dramatic. I'm afraid it might also become monotonous. How can I "jazz up" this two-color scheme for a living room? How do I introduce just enough of other colors and still keep a black and white room?*

Try mixing flowered prints and bold plaids in just two colors for excitement and drama.

Variety in pattern can make a black and white color scheme striking. Use a black and white plaid on your couch, and a black and white flowered print on facing club chairs. Hang white window draperies with borders of the flowered print. The rug can be white with flecks of black. For your third color, use lots of green plants in white pots. On a white coffee table place accessories in bright yellows and reds.

20

The Living Room

Question: *I decorated my living room about a year ago, and I'm afraid I went overboard for green. I have an olive green sofa with red figures, and an olive green chair, wall-to-wall carpeting, a light green and brown recliner and draperies. All I can see now is green which is getting sickening. Please tell me what I can do to get some of this green out of my hair. My walls and ceiling are off-white.*

Monochromatic decorating schemes are monotonous.

I can certainly understand why you are bored with your living room. There is no room in a house that should be decorated in only one color. To redecorate your living room, you won't need to start from scratch. Leave your olive green carpeting; it would be too expensive to change. Leave your green and red sofa, too. Slipcover your olive green chair with a gold, red and off-white striped fabric. Use gold, red and off-white pillows on your sofa. Definitely change the draperies. I would suggest off-white draperies with a gold trim under a gold valance. If money permits, re-cover your recliner in a gold nylon fabric.

Question: *We are building a new home and need help with the living room. The walls will all be white. We have a sectional sofa which I would like to do over; we also have two barrel chairs covered in soft turquoise, and two blue lamps that are the same shade of turquoise. I want to know what colors we should choose for wall-to-wall carpeting and draperies? We have several bristol blue ashtrays.*

Soft champagne works with white and blue for serenity—watermelon adds juicy spice.

I would recommend a soft champagne carpeting for your living room, and for all of your new home, if you wish, for it blends with everything and is serviceable. In your living room hang beige draperies under a watermelon-colored valance. Line the valance in a soft blue, gold and white stripe fabric, and recover your sectional sofa in the same fabric. Use watermelon red throw pillows on the sofa for accent. The watermelon and beige colors will look lovely with soft turquoise and bristol blue.

Question: *The walls, draperies and carpet of our living room are all beige. The sofa is a beige tapestry and the two occasional chairs are a pale orange olive mixture. Please tell me how to brighten up the room without spending very much money.*

New valances, pillows and green plants are an inexpensive way to brighten a living room.

You have a problem with all that beige, but you can solve it easily and inexpensively. Hang a bright cantaloupe, tangy orange and lemon print valance as a glowing halo at the top of your beige draperies. Line the valance in olive and trim the sides of your draperies with the olive also. Sparkle up your sofa with some bright pillows—lemon, cantaloupe, olive—and a pillow or two of the new valance fabric. For additional brightening effects, use lots of green plants throughout the room. Finally, consider a colorful rug for right under your coffee table, perhaps yellow with an orange border.

Question: *My living room, which overlooks a lake, is paneled in cherry. The carpeting is avocado green; the sofa is moss green and gold. I have a lounge chair upholstered in toast and two occasional chairs covered in pale honey. I have very full sheer white curtains on a large picture window. What can I do to give this room a little lift? I have a wall mirror framed in mahogany. Should I paint it?*

When decorating a dark-paneled room, use bright colorful fabrics.

Your room surely needs a lift, but simply painting the mirror frame won't do the job. Why not slipcover your lounge chair in a great orange, avocado, sky blue, gold and geranium red floral print on a white background and the occasional chairs in an avocado and gold stripe? Put big pillows of the lounge chair print with fluted borders on the sofa. Hang a bright gold valance at your picture window over the white sheer curtains and line it with the print you use on your lounge chair. Buy some bright canary yellow lamps with white shades for your room. Fill the room with lots of country garden plants in white hobnail pots, or hang some plants in natural clay pots on your cherry walls. Paint your mirror frame a bright sunny yellow—the same color yellow as the base of your lamps.

Question: *Our couch is chocolate brown, and two chairs are beige naugahyde. I like them but would like to provide a colorful setting for them. How do you make conservative brown and beige seem exciting and gay?*

For the young at heart—plum, zinnia, red and white will make a brown and beige living room come alive.

Brown and beige are perfect foils for some of the modern colors being used in decorating. Paint your walls a vibrant plum color. Toss some zinnia red pillows on your couch. Some bright white is needed in this setting, and I recommend a white fur area rug beneath a stainless steel coffee table. An abstract painting with a white background would look great over your couch.

Question: *I recently bought a lovely yellow carpet for our living room. Our draperies are a floral print of yellow, orange and mint green on a white background. I'd like to slipcover our couch and chair, which are now a dark green. Do I have to stay with solid colors?*

The stripe is the decorating common denominator. It works with everything.

Why not use a yellow, black, paprika orange and white stripe on your couch? Cover your chair with the floral print of your draperies, and cover a pull-up chair with the same stripe which is on the couch. Summertime yellow walls would unify your cheerful room.

The Living Room

Question: *We are each 70 years old. We just sold our home of 33 years and are going into a new condominium. Would you give me some help in doing a lively and colorful living room? All we have to start with is a beautiful shag carpet in a dark green. I hate to rely on my decorating ideas of 30 years ago. This is our last chance to put some spice into our lives.*

Parsons tables are a big decorative favorite—and an inexpensive one.

If spice is what you want, you will have it—and I'm all for making this world as beautiful and happy and colorful as it can be. Why not paint your walls a sunny yellow with white ceiling and trim? Use a melon, pink, geranium red, delphinium blue and emerald green floral print at your windows under a matching valance. Find a sofa in solid melon and accent it with print pillows to match your curtains. A very modern, very practical thing to buy would be white Parsons tables; use them at each end of your sofa, and some bright green ginger-jar lamps with white shades. Use a deep forest green and white print on your club chairs and sunny yellow on an occasional chair or two. Bring some of your accessories with you—books, plant stands, china, ashtrays, etc. I believe your new home should be a collection of the past things you love, the present things you like and your dreams for the future. Seventy is not old.

Question: *Our living room sofa is orange, medium brown and dark brown plaid. The chair is orange and brown tweed. I find myself at a total loss as to what colors to use for walls, draperies, carpet and sofa pillows. The furniture is colonial design. We want our room to look cozy and comfortable.*

Though wall trim is often painted white, a striking look can be achieved by painting the trim a rich dark color and the walls a light warm tone.

I think you should begin by painting your walls the color of yummy cream, and the trim a rich chocolate brown semigloss enamel. Then look for a plaid carpet—one that has a cream-colored ground with chocolate brown, rust and emerald green blocks. For draperies I'd pick a handsome cream-colored linen and line it in emerald green. For accent pillows, use sky blue, emerald green and lemon yellow.

Question: *My carpet is a very dark gold, the walls are light gold with gold and white stripe vinyl wallpaper on the end wall. Draperies are the same gold as the walls. What color and fabric should I have for a sofa, two wing chairs and an occasional chair? I would like to carry out the country-French look.*

French blue and white toile will achieve the country-French look.

So far, you have only gold in your living room. Why not use a French blue and white cotton toile de Jouy pattern for your sofa and the occasional chair? Wing chairs can be in French blue, geranium pink, gold and white plaid linen. Put lots of buttercup yellow, geranium pink and grass green throw pillows on your sofa. A black pole lamp with deep blue drum shade would be great next to your sofa.

Question: *We just bought gold carpeting for the living room, which we want to complete in gold, red orange, white and black or brown. Could you advise me how to distribute these colors among draperies, sofa, two chairs and walls?*

Gold living room carpeting calls for chocolate walls with white trim.

Why not color your walls a chocolate brown with white woodwork and white ceiling? Use orange, brown, green and gold on a clean white background on your sofa. Your club chairs can be hot red orange. Draperies can be sparkling white under a valance of the print to match your sofa. Line the valance in gold.

Question: *Would you please tell me what color rug to get for my living room? I have light beige walls. My living room suite is covered in brown with a little silver fleck. One chair is rust. Draperies are beige olive.*

Bright red, olive green, champagne beige and chocolate brown is a singing, sunny color scheme.

Rather dreary! Beige, brown, olive and rust together hardly sing of a country garden. Buy a rich bright red carpet, but the carpet alone will not brighten up your living room. Add some bright red and olive green throw pillows to that brown sofa and slipcover your rust chair with a red, olive and brown print on a white background. A valance of the sparkling print over your olive draperies would also brighten the room.

Question: *Will you please tell me what color slipcovers I could buy for my living room furniture, which consists of two couches and two chairs? Also, what color should I consider for draperies? The walls are painted white, and the wall-to-wall carpeting is speckled red, white and black.*

White walls are usually a safe, sure bet.

White walls are fine—most people have them—but all the more reason for adding dramatic colors to your living room. Red, white and black is a great decorating scheme, so why not go that route? Slipcover your two sofas in a black-on-white damask design. The chairs can be slipcovered in bright red. Use red and white pillows on the sofas. White lamps with black shades would be a further decorating plus in your setting.

Question: *My living room walls are white. I have an olive green traditional sofa, two Italian provincial accent chairs in gold shantung, an Italian coffee table and end tables. On the end tables there are brass lamps with white shades. I would appreciate your ideas for another chair, a rug and draperies.*

Red wall-to-wall carpeting brightens and unifies a green and gold living room.

Your room needs a good lift. Why not use a bright red wall-to-wall carpeting on the floor with an Oriental rug under your coffee table? Red and gold pillows would improve the look of your olive green sofa. I would hang trellis design gold-on-white draperies at the window. Your new chair might be covered in a traditional gold, red and olive green cut velvet.

Question: *Our modern living room furniture has frames of warm rosewood. Two barrel chairs are covered in black naugahyde; the sofa is covered in beige and white tweed. We need color ideas for walls, curtains and rug.*

For the sophisticated modern look, a black, brown and white living room is the answer.

Soft cocoa brown walls provide an extremely modern look that isn't at all stark. Your curtains can be soft white. For a touch of the safari—a black and white zebra area rug on a pearl gray carpet would be the dramatic focal point of the room.

Question: *Our living room has a built-in corner cabinet which we want to highlight. It is white now, as are the walls. Do we dare paint the cabinet, and if so, what color? Our sofa is solid red, and two wing chairs are a red, yellow and green floral print.*

Bright red and sunny yellow is a winning color combination for a living room.

Paint the woodwork in your living room a sunny yellow and leave your walls sparkling white. To show up the corner cabinet, paint the inside of the piece a bright red, the rest of it the sunny yellow of the woodwork.

Question: *I would like to redecorate our living room by slipcovering our Italian provincial couch and two traditional chairs. Our draperies are a gold floral print on a white background. The carpeting is sandalwood, and the walls are off-white; neither can be changed as we live in an apartment. What colors do you suggest for the couch and two chairs? Friends have suggested green, but somehow it sounds dull.*

Slipcovers are the inexpensive way to bring color to a living room. They can change the total color scheme and do not cost as much as reupholstery and carpeting.

Your friends may be giving you good advice. Bright emerald green slipcovers on your two traditional chairs would be fine. Slipcover your couch in an emerald green, gold and white stripe. If you have some of your gold and white flowered drapery material on hand, use it for sofa pillow accents; if not, I'd suggest rich melon and lettuce green pillows on your sofa. Lots of green ferns and plants in bright brass tubs would add real freshness to the room.

Question: *I have just moved into a new apartment. My living room suite consists of a black and muted gold sofa, a sand-color chair and a muted gold chair. I must buy draperies, rugs and some tables. What colors would you use for these and what color would you paint the walls?*

If a living room suite is predominantly gold, bring color into your life with a green rug and floral curtains.

You seem to like the gold tones, so I would suggest that you paint your walls a rich gold with white ceiling and woodwork. Then, for sparkle and color contrast, at your windows hang draperies of a colorful floral print featuring emerald greens, bright golds, oranges and reds on a white background. I think you should slipcover your sand-color chair with the same print fabric you use for draperies. Put two round red throw pillows on the sofa and perhaps, if money holds out, add two 16-inch-square pillows of the drapery print. Use a bright emerald green rug in your room. End tables might be white, or red lacquer; if you prefer wood tables, select honey fruitwood.

30

Question: *For the living room of the new house we are building we have purchased royal blue carpeting and white draperies. The walls will be white. My husband and I love bright, contrasting colors, and are open to suggestions for a living room color scheme.*

Orange and blue, on opposite sides of the color wheel, are complementary, stimulating colors to emphasize in a living room.

If you like contrast, try a festive print of blues and orange on the sofa. A lounge chair can be orange; occasional chairs can be covered in light blue. This should give you a nice balance with the blue carpet and white draperies and walls. Add fresh green plants and accessories for excitement.

Question: *My living room carpeting is pearl gray and the walls are white. Our furniture is rather traditional. I'd like to use the new plums and purples in the room, and am thinking of new draperies in a plum, purple, emerald green and white stripe. Can I use these colors on a Chippendale sofa? Should I change the wall color?*

Modern color schemes mix well with traditional furnishings.

Don't ever be afraid to use modern colors in a traditional or formal setting. Your new drapery colors sound just right. In fact, you should use the same fabric to cover your sofa. Cover a pull-up chair with plum or purple and lacquer the frame emerald green. I'd paint the walls a pearl gray with white woodwork and ceiling to provide a contrasting background for your new colors. On the pearl gray wall over the sofa, hang a magenta and red modern painting.

The Living Room

Question: *In our living room there is an olive green couch, his-and-her chairs covered with a beige-on-eggshell damask fabric, and mahogany end tables and coffee table. What colors should I use for walls, draperies, rug and accessories? I am considering either panels or paint for the walls.*

Lemon yellow works as well for most walls as white.

Your room needs a lift! Yellow, if it is kept soft, is an excellent and exciting background color and so is soft blue. Almost anything goes with these two; I wish more people would consider yellow or blue walls instead of white. Paint your walls a soft lemon yellow with lots of white trim. For your floor, I would recommend cerulean blue carpeting, and at the windows, a bright gay print featuring daffodil yellow, hot orange, brilliant green and sky blue flowers on a white background. Use daffodil yellow and sky blue pillows on the olive green sofa. Bright yellow lamps and accessories would help your room, as would a club chair and ottoman covered in the print to match your curtains.

Question: *My sofa and one chair are a pumpkin pie gold brown tweed and another chair is olive green. One wall is fully draped in olive green and the other walls are paneled in light birch. What color carpet should I invest in? I am considering changing the draperies, and if I do, what color should they be?*

Decorate a room around your favorite season of the year.

It sounds as though you enjoy the blazing colors of the autumn season. For your new carpet, I would choose a rich gold or a spicy russet. You should definitely change your draperies. For one thing, you have too much olive green in the living room; for another, your room is in need of a print. For the draperies, select a bright print in gold, melon, orange red, yellow, lettuce green and olive on a light beige background; in other words, look for a print that reminds you of a New England tree-covered hill in October! Hang the draperies under an olive valance lined with gold. Use the print on an occasional chair, a hassock or throw pillows for the sofa.

Question: *Our new condominium apartment has gold carpeting and white walls. I want to know what colors to choose for the furniture and draperies in the living room. There is a pass-through window from the living room to the kitchen. I want to put up shutters at the window, but need to know what color. Please give me advice on lamps, too, as I never have any original ideas about them.*

Lamp shades made of a colorful print to match your draperies are young, bright and fun.

I would look for a gold, yellow and green floral print for your living room window draperies. Then, I'd repeat the print on two club chairs, and on lampshades which have white ironstone bases. Find a sofa in a bright blue and white stripe. On the sofa place throw pillows having the same print as the draperies, chairs, and lamp shades. I would use bright marine blue louvered shutters at your pass-through window.

Question: *My living room is dull. The walls are light tan with off-white woodwork. On avocado green carpeting, I have placed a green sofa and one white chair. I have two beautiful lamps with a design of daisies and green ferns on the bases and white shades. The draperies are a brown and orange print on an off-white background. What should I do to make the room brighter?*

The color scheme of a prized possession—such as a vase, lamp or needlepoint chair—may give you ideas for color for an entire room.

Take your cue from your daisy and fern lamp bases, and begin a colorful scheme. Oftentimes the happiest combination of colors is right under your nose. You love the white, yellow and green on your lamps, so let's give these outdoor colors the natural and best background for them. I would start by painting the walls a pale sky blue and the woodwork white semigloss enamel. If you can afford to replace the draperies, this would be a tremendous lift for your room. Select a daisy yellow, fern green, and sky blue print on a white background; your avocado rug and your draperies will look livelier—and so will your white chair. Use some throw pillows on your sofa of the curtain print and also some bright sunny yellow ones.

34

The Living Room

Question: *We have an English camel back sofa in our living room of which we're very proud, but I am tired of its rather dull beige upholstery. I'd like to know if I could cover it in red. We have an Oriental rug with a marvelous bright red in it that I'd like to match.*

A camel-back sofa in bright red is a dramatic note in a traditional living room.

By all means, cover your camel back sofa in the bright red of your rug. For heightened drama, use the same fabric for window draperies and valances.

Question: *Our living room has emerald green carpeting, gold and beige furniture, and white draperies and walls. I know this is a perfectly acceptable color scheme, but to me it has become uninteresting. What would you suggest for a dramatic change? I'd like to keep the carpeting.*

Change the colors of a room's fabrics and you change the whole mood of the room.

A floral pattern of lavender, plum, and emerald green on a white background would be a springtime sensation at the windows in your living room. Your sofa covered in a bright white and the chairs in a rich plum would be lovely on the emerald green carpet. Use plum or purple pillows on the sofa, and see how your new colors welcome and cheer you!

36

The Living Room

Question: *In my living room I have warm yellow shag wall-to-wall carpeting. My draperies are a yellow sheer. A traditional sofa is off-white crushed velvet, and on two contemporary swivel chairs I have used a soft white and yellow fabric. Against the long living room wall I have a large black Parsons table 10 feet long on which I have placed a 48-inch-high silver lamp with white shade. What end tables would you use on each side of the sofa? I am thinking of black tables and want to know if two more black tables would be too much.*

Every room needs a touch of black.

Your room sounds very attractive. I have always believed that every room needs a touch of black, be that touch a Parsons table or a lampshade. I would not object to black end tables, provided you use some attractive lemon yellow, white, and green Oriental style lamp bases with white shades. I'd like to see you use a pair of pull-out benches under your long black Parsons table. The benches could be covered in a soft green and white stripe. I'd also like to see lots of pillows on your sofa in various shades of green: kelly green, apple green, mint green and palest pale of the greens. I also hope you use lots of live green plants in the living room.

Question: *My living room is done in fruitwood Italian provincial. My couch is peacock blue and I have two high-back chairs upholstered in red. I have recently purchased some round marble-top tables. My walls are white. What colors should I use for draperies, rug, and accessories?*

Peacock blue, red and white is a bold and effective color scheme.

Peacock blue and red with white walls is not a timid combination. I like it. What about a peacock blue and white damask fabric for your draperies under a peacock blue swag-and-jabot valance? Line the swags and jabots with white. Carpet for your room should be red, and I would use red and white throw pillows on your peacock blue sofa. White opaline lamps with white shades would be handsome in your room, as would an ashtray or two and a cigarette box in peacock blue.

Question: *My husband and I will soon be moving into student housing, a situation common to many couples. The floors are bare, walls are white, and white draperies are furnished. I would like to plan the living room around a large blue velvet sofa and a chair in a print of bronze, dark green, orange and blue on beige, which we picked up at an auction. Can you suggest a color for a new rug, as well as ideas for a dining set which will have to go in the living room corner? We'd like something modern.*

A bright orange area rug can be used in future home decorating as well as in today's student apartment.

In your new student housing apartment, I'd select a bright orange carpet, an area carpet that you can take with you when you move. I've had student apartments myself, and know you might use the rug in a child's room one day. Indeed, if you dig modern furniture, go that route for your dining set. Ice cream parlor chairs with white lacquered frames and royal blue naugahyde seats would be great around a white mushroom-base table. Bright orange, canary yellow and emerald green would be my suggestion for throw pillows on your blue velvet sofa. A lot of personally selected prints of modern paintings would enhance your setting.

Question: *We are going to almost completely redecorate our living room, which has gold wall-to-wall carpeting and one wall paneled in maple. We are keeping one brown leather chair and a beautiful green lamp. What colors do you suggest for walls, draperies, sofa and a new chair?*

Sky blue is the most neutral of the colors. Just as it works as a background for a total universe, so it will work with every color in your living room.

I would begin with pale sky blue walls and lots of white trim. Your draperies can be a sky blue, chocolate brown, gold, and bright green print hung under a green valance. I would use a gold sofa in the room with pillows of the sky blue and green. Your new chair can be covered in the drapery print. On your maple paneled wall I would hang lots of fresh green plants in natural earthenware pots.

38

The Living Room

Question: *The living room of our new apartment has a northern exposure and, as a result, does not get very much light. We start with a brown couch, a cocoa covered ottoman, and a glass-top coffee table. What colors do you recommend for walls, draperies, and a pull-up chair?*

Green and white trellis wallpaper and matching draperies bring airiness to a living room that receives little sunlight.

Your brown and cocoa colors will show up beautifully against a nature green and white trellis design wall covering. Use a coordinating fabric for the draperies and one or two pull-up chairs. In this setting, I would like to see a zebra rug under a glass coffee table to add the unexpected touch to the room. An abstract painting featuring rich mandarin orange would look sensational over your couch.

Question: *I have a sofa alcove in my living room that I'd like to dramatize. What colors should I paint the alcove and the rest of the walls? My straight-line sofa is covered in vanilla naugahyde; two steel-framed chairs are charcoal gray naugahyde; a third chair is beige leather. I have white cube end tables inside the alcove with the sofa.*

Lemon and lime are delicious sherbets—and delicious decorating colors, too.

I'd suggest a lemon and white bamboo pattern vinyl for the walls of your living room. The sofa alcove walls can be painted a rich lime sherbet color. Paint the cube end tables lemon yellow, and accent your sofa with bright lemon pillows. Nature's green plants would add a nice outdoor touch to the top of your coffee table.

40

The Living Room

Question: *My furniture is Early American. The couch is orange, one chair is a darker orange and the other chair is a patchwork pattern mostly in shades of brown, orange and gold. The walls are off-white with one wall paneled in dark wood. The carpeting is furnished, but I have a choice of gold or dark emerald green shag; which color would you choose? What color draperies do you suggest?*

Combine floral prints with patchwork for the warm, cheerful look an Early American living room deserves.

Since your carpet choice is limited, I would recommend the gold. Hang cheerful print curtains at your windows. A flowered design of oranges, emerald greens, yellows and royal blues on a white background would be my choice. Use pillows of the print for accent on your orange couch. I like the use of flowered prints and patchwork, as long as their colors work together.

Question: *My husband and I have just purchased an old farmhouse which we would like to remodel. I have my heart set on painting the living room walls a flat red or orange. Then I'd like to cover the sofa in an oyster color, and perhaps the chairs in a gold print. The rug is a neutral fringed print, rather faded. Would red walls be too overwhelming in this high-ceiling 15-by-13 room? Also, we need a new rug, preferably a print, but can we put print chairs on a print rug? I like the eclectic look!*

This is the age of the pattern-on-pattern rage. Just be sure the colors live well together.

By all means paint your walls red—a soft tomato red with lots of bright white semigloss enamel for the trim. An oyster white textured fabric for the sofa sounds great. For the two chairs I'd find something more dramatic than a gold print. Why not choose a Moroccan or flamestitch patterned fabric in red, orange, earth brown and white? A new rug could be a Moroccan or geometric print in bright white, tomato red, apricot orange, earth brown, sunshine yellow and Christmas green. Don't be afraid of mixing patterns, as long as the colors are harmonious.

Question: *Our large living room has solid oak woodwork finished in medium dark varnish. There is lots of woodwork with wide baseboards. I would like to have a blue room with gold accents. Should I paint the woodwork blue or leave it as it is?*

Think twice before painting over beautiful woodwork. Wood is a color.

Please leave your solid oak woodwork alone. Use blue curtains at your windows and trim the curtains in your desired gold. Select a blue or gold rug for your room, and use blue and gold fabric on your furniture, but leave the oak paneling as it is. I envy you.

Question: *My new living room walls are painted dove beige, and the carpet is gold beige. I already have a pair of French provincial chairs in blue. What color should a new sofa be?*

Red does wonders in a gold and blue living room.

Brilliant red would be my suggestion for your sofa. Use throw pillows on the sofa, some blue ones and some gold ones. Find blue pillows close in color to your blue French provincial chairs. I'd like to see draperies in a gay print of golds, blues and reds at your windows under a bright red valance.

The Dining Room

Dash up your dining room! How can anyone enjoy eating in a stuffy dining room? I have seen some very handsome traditional dining rooms across the country, and I have seen some mighty dreary ones. Dreariness is not determined by style of furniture as some people would have you believe.

If you have a bent for the traditional, think how exciting your mahogany furniture would look in a lemon yellow and white setting. Enhance the charm of a French provincial dining room with gingham checks. Show off your modern dining set against a scheme of clean, clear colors: lemon yellow, emerald green, shocking pink, and white.

Is yours the dining room designed for formal, stately dining, the paneled room that calls for rich colors in brocade or velvet? Perhaps yours is the warm, friendly room in which the kids congregate to do their homework and friends sit around in to visit or play cards as well as to eat; if so, you may be looking for sturdy, practical furnishings in gay colors and prints.

Dining rooms are frequently small rooms. But any room can be "enlarged" with strategic use of the right colors. Dining rooms, in particular, are often visually "expanded" or "opened up" with wall mirrors or trompe l'oeil wallpaper.

For many people, today's dining room is an area off the living room; this is especially true for apartment dwellers. The two areas can be coordinated in their colors, but, for heaven's sake, do not let a department store retailer convince you that furniture for the living room and dining room must match. Matching living room and dining room furnishings will give you an unfortunate look of overcoordination and lack of imagination and daring!

If you have a mahogany Queen Anne living room, there is no reason whatever why you can't have a dining room styled with painted pieces of furniture. For instance, the living room color scheme is gold and pumpkin with avocado accents. You could paint the frames of dining chairs a rich avocado lacquer. Upholster the seats of the chairs in a bright pumpkin and beige tweed. Your dining room curtains can be an avocado, orange and white geometric print, and they can be hung on a walnut- or mahogany-stained pole, of course with mahogany- or walnut-stained rings. I'd use a beige area rug with a pumpkin or avocado border. I like rugs that have borders. It gives them a satisfying, finished look.

Speaking of rugs in the dining room, why not use a rug to bring a multicolor pattern to the floor? The days of plain Jane rugs under the dining table are gone; pattern on pattern is the rage. When selecting a dining room rug, think pattern: geometric, trellis, stripe, floral. When buying a dining room rug, be sure it is wide enough and long enough. The back legs of the dining room chairs should be on the rug when the chairs are occupied.

There is in America a group of people, numbering in the millions, who like serenity in dining. These people search for the mellow look, oftentimes called the restful feeling. It's only natural. Dad comes home from a busy day at the shop or office. Mom cooks, cleans and chauffeurs the kids all day. The wise decorator understands the working situations of the family members. If your family is active by day, why not consider a mellow restful dining room decor? Eating will be that much more pleasant and relaxing. Paint your walls the softest beige, all your wood-work the crispest white. The other colors can be gold, avocado and chocolate brown. The furniture can be mahogany, walnut or fruitwood. These are soft, easy-to-live-with colors. But it's not a dull, washed-out scheme.

Lighting is of the utmost importance in creating a restful dining room setting. I strongly recommend crystal, if the budget allows. Another possibility for a restful setting is a brass hurricane-type fixture, not with hurricane globes, but with clear translucent shades made of fabric. And, of course, candlelight for restful dining is a must. Many women, and men too, think candlelight is pretentious. Phooey on this idea! Candle-light rests the eyes and the soul. Besides, someday candlelight dining might be less expensive than dining by electric light.

Lots of people like dining rooms filled with bright colors. This makes sense, as a good chef knows when planning a complete meal. The cook knows that diners respond well to meals that are color-planned as care-fully as taste-planned. Who wants white fish, white mashed potatoes and white creamed onions on his dinner plate? Bland-looking dishes never have stimulated the appetite, so why expect a bland dining room to do the job? Put colorful food on the dinner plate—carrots or tomato slices, some rich green asparagus, some yellow corn with pimiento accents—

and the mouth waters. Add some strawberry pink, lemon yellow, pistachio green to a bland dining room and the spirit soars.

Because it is not a room in which you spend the greater part of your day, the dining room may be just the room for that extra bold, truly dramatic color scheme that might be too much to live with for long periods. Did you ever long for really red, red, walls, but were afraid to try red in the living room or bedroom? Or any other colors you felt would be "inappropriate" in the other rooms? Here's your chance! Too many people do not want to take the time to live. They rush through life thinking that each meal is a chore, a must, a thing to be gotten over fast in order to allow time for the next thing. These poor people are losing life by reaching always for the thing beyond that may or may not exist, at the expense of enjoying and making the most of the pleasures at hand each day. A homemaker who really cares about living, and values being alive, will set a colorful table. And I don't mean that a table has to be set with the finest china and the most expensive porcelain figurine centerpiece.

I love a dining table set with the most natural colors and textures. Try a placemat on your table of natural green spring leaves or of autumn foliage. The plates can sit on natural leaves as well as they can sit on pure Irish linen. Colored paper napkins tied with a colorful yarn bow can make a table setting exciting. And I am all for crockery plates and crockery clay soup bowls with their brown tops. Earthenware table settings are delightful.

While I love fresh flowers, I do not believe that flowers are the only centerpieces available for the dining room table. Why not try a piece of sculpture as a centerpiece, or a handsome figurine, or a glass statue? You can use a clay pot filled with a handsome geranium, or a spray of feathers. You can create a centerpiece with fruits and dried berries, or you can make a centerpiece of miniature furniture. For Sis's birthday party, her dollhouse would make a charming center attraction. Centerpieces are for attraction and interest and to stimulate conversation as much as they are for beauty. Yes, there are many ways to make a dining room colorful and exciting, but there is no more important way than top-of-the-table planning.

Question: *I am about to redecorate my living room and dining room, which are adjoining. I want new carpeting, draperies and wall paint. I have a pink sofa and two aqua and white chairs in my living room, and a French provincial dining room set. What color carpeting, walls and draperies do you suggest for both rooms?*

A simple, soft floral pattern can be used in living-dining room wall-to-wall carpeting.

I love a floral pattern in carpeting, and your colors suggest this is the pattern for you. Look for a sunshine yellow background and small white flowers with rose pink centers. I suggest you paint your walls a pale sunshine yellow with white semigloss enamel for the trim. Draperies can be bright white cotton fabric with a rose pink, aqua, and sunshine yellow trim down the front and across the bottom. Put lots of emerald green, aqua and melon throw pillows on your pink sofa.

Question: *Our dining room needs some redecorating, but I'm not sure what to redecorate. We definitely need a new carpet—not too light in color because of our young children. The walls are beige. The draperies are a dark brown linen texture over bright yellow sheer curtains. The dining room chair seats are royal blue. I have been hoping that all we need to change is the carpet and the chair seats. Can you suggest the right, but* practical, *colors?*

Practical fabrics do not need to be drab colors.

How about a geometric print for your chair seats, perhaps shocking pink, lemon yellow and lime green on a chocolate brown background. What could be more practical and yet alive? If possible you might put a three-inch border of the same fabric down the front panels of your draperies. Your new carpet can be a chocolate brown and white shag tweed. Lemon yellow, shocking pink and lime green accents in your table settings would be great. Be daring and use color—you only live once.

Question: *My modern dining room set is white: a round pedestal table and swivel chairs. The floor is white vinyl. What colors can I put on the walls and chair seats to make the room interesting?*

A star-spangled decorating scheme of red, white and blue is both vibrant and soothing for dining.

Try a patriotic decorating scheme in your dining room: bright red walls with your white furniture and white floor; bright blue upholstery on the white swivel chairs. Colorful modern paintings on the red walls would add to the excitement. So would a mirror in an antique brass or gold leaf frame and a brass chandelier.

Question: *What color should I paint my dining room walls? The carpet is rose beige, and the draperies are white. How else might I get color into the room—in addition to painting the walls.*

Snap up a dining room decor with colorful valances.

For wall coloring in your dining room, consider champagne beige with lots of white trim. Then top your white draperies with valances in a salmon pink, white and chocolate brown stripe. You might also consider using the stripe on the seats of your dining chairs. Set your table with bright emerald green placemats and salmon napkins.

Question: *We just moved into a new home, and I want everything just so! I have a French provincial living room set. Must I buy French provincial furniture for the dining room, which opens right off the living room, or can I mix and buy Spanish or Italian? Also, must my draperies in the living room and dining room match?*

Dining room and living room furniture does not have to match; use color to coordinate the rooms.

Living room furniture does not have to match dining room furniture, even if rooms run together. In fact, I love the mixed look! Mix the old and the new, different styles of furniture and different kinds of woods. I suggest you coordinate the two rooms by using the same colors in both living room and dining room draperies. However, drapery patterns do not need to match.

Question: *My dining room walls are avocado green, and the trim is white. We have maple furniture and a brass ceiling lantern. I want to buy new curtains for two windows. What would you suggest?*

Documentary print fabrics add distinction to colonial dining rooms.

Obviously you like a colonial look, so why not use a documentary print café-style drapery on brass poles at your windows? There are many Americana prints in a wide variety of colors on the market, and I'm certain you'll find one that will suit your decorating fancy. Frankly, I'd like to see you select a print with lots of orange, beige, sunny yellow and avocado green on a white background.

Question: *Three walls in our dining room are Italian straw with a tint of green; the other wall is done in walnut paneling. The carpeting is yellow, green and blue tweed. What colors should I consider for new draperies and dining room chair covers? We have a large still-life picture done in yellow and green in a bright green frame.*

Add zip to your dining room with a shocking pink and yellow color scheme.

How about an Oriental patterned drapery fabric? The background could be Ming yellow with lots of fern green, mulberry, mauve pink, chocolate brown, royal blue and cantaloupe orange. Cover your chair seats in a shocking pink. Placemats can be Ming yellow with fern green napkins.

Question: *We need something to tie our living and dining rooms together. They are separated only by a large arch, so colors should blend. Colors in the living room include mostly gold-upholstered furniture, with touches of antique white and olive green. In both living and dining rooms the draperies are off-white brocade, carpeting is nutria. The dining room set is mahogany. What colors can I consider for the seats of dining room chairs and the dining room wall?*

Velvety cantaloupe will tie together a dining room with a gold and white living room.

Cantaloupe is the color for you. Use a cantaloupe fabric on your dining room chairs. Put a few cantaloupe and white striped pillows on the living room sofa. I would paint the dining room walls a soft gold, with white trim and ceiling. Consider valances of a floral pattern in cantaloupe, olive green and white for both living room and dining room windows.

Question: *Our small dining room has brick-patterned vinyl on the floors, and the walls are white. The buffet top is melon laminated plastic, and the round wrought-iron table top is white laminate. Should I paint the buffet sides melon? They are now white, but I would like more color and cheer in the room. What kind and color of curtains would you recommend for one fairly large window?*

People love to eat outdoors, so why not bring the look of a patio into a dining room?

With your brick floor, white walls and wrought-iron table, you are well on your way to achieving that patio look that people love for eating. I suggest you increase the feel of summer by hanging café curtains of a floral pattern in poppy orange and leaf green on a white background. You should leave the sides of your buffet white to give the room an illusion of being larger. For additional color, paint the wrought-iron table base a rich green. Cover chairs in bright orange.

50

Question: *I have inherited beautiful walnut chairs, a table and a breakfront for my dining room. There is also a beige rug, but this is all I have. What colors should I consider for the walls, curtains and the chair coverings?*

Autumnal colors go especially well with traditional dining room furniture.

First, paint your walls pumpkin with white trim. Hang a pumpkin fabric roller shade at your window. Cover the seats of your dining chairs with champagne beige and pumpkin tweed fabric. Fill your breakfront with china in an ivy green and white pattern.

Question: *We are moving into a small 75-year-old farmhouse. The dining room window treatment has me stumped. The east wall has one double-hung window and a door opening onto an enclosed sun-porch. The west wall has two double-hung windows side by side. The view is beautiful everywhere. What should be done to the window and door in the east wall so that they will be attractive from both dining room and porch?*

When a dining room is connected to a porch, use sunny, natural colors to achieve the feeling of one big outdoor room.

I suggest you treat the three windows the same by using white louvered shutters on all. Be sure to use shutters on the porch side of the window, too. When the shutters are open, as they will be most of the time, your view will be the same from either side. As for the door, I would leave it alone; you might even remove it. To continue the effect of one big indoor-outdoor room, why not panel the bottom half of the dining room, with a chair rail, and paint paneling and rail a white? Paper the walls above the chair rail in a trellis-type pattern of fern green and white or lemon yellow and white. Dining room chair seats can be covered in a brilliant mauve pink.

Question: *The walls in our living room/dining room combination are white. We have off-white draperies with an antique gold print. I have picked out a turquoise living room set. The chairs of my dining set are upholstered in an antique gold and brighter gold fabric. Please tell me what color wall-to-wall carpeting will go with this combination of colors.*

Turquoise, green, white and gold make a beautiful living-dining room color scheme.

My suggestion would be a rich emerald green carpeting. This will go well with the golds in your dining room set. Then you should unify the colors in your living room by putting lots of emerald green, white and gold pillows on your sofa. An orange pillow tossed in for good measure would be an eye catcher.

Question: *My dining room has emerald green carpeting and a dining set in black lacquer with a walnut table top. I'd appreciate your color suggestions for the walls and curtains to cover a sliding door.*

A successful color scheme can be achieved by repeating the same color—but in different shades.

If green is your color, paint your dining room walls a light apple green with white trim. Hang sheer white curtains under draperies in a floral pattern of paprika orange and several shades of green on a white background. Cover chair seats with the same fabric. If you have a recessed wall space with shelves for china, paint the interior an emerald green to match your carpet; paint the shelves white.

Question: *Our living room, with its barn red and white toile wallpaper above a white dado, is visible from the dining room. So is the mustard and white papered front hall. Could you suggest a warm color scheme for our still bare dining room? Something that won't clash with the hall and living room, please.*

Barn red fabric for walls brings an elegant tone to a dining room.

Why not cover the wall with a solid barn red fabric or flocked wallpaper? Paint your trim off-white. Draperies can be a lemony gold damask. Dining chair seats can be the same color damask as the drapery, or they can be a deep monarch green. You should hang some interesting, lighted oil paintings on your barn red walls and a handsome crystal and bronze fixture over your table. I would recommend an Oriental rug for the floor under your table.

Question: *My dining room is a small room. The furniture is mahogany, carpeting and draperies are solid royal blue, and walls are white. What color should I use for chair seats?*

Don't overdo blue in a dining room.

Believe it or not, blue is a color that doesn't go well with food. Some blue in a dining room is fine, but you definitely need to introduce another color, perhaps lime green. Upholster your dining room chair seats in a lime green patent vinyl. Placemats can be lime green with royal blue napkins. Water goblets might be cranberry red.

Question: *We are going to carpet the dining room in a rich red. The walls and trim are white. What colors do you suggest for draperies and reupholstered dining room chairs?*

If you use a washable suede vinyl on the seats of your dining room chairs, you are free to use bright colors.

I urge you to consider vinyl upholstery; it's no trouble to keep clean, and you can use the brightest, clearest colors. Your dining room chairs should be covered with brilliant lemon yellow suede vinyl. A red and white linen damask-type fabric would be perfect for draperies. Use touches of fern green in your table accessories, or hang a potted fern or two in windows.

Question: *We have a traditional dining room. The English chairs have ball-and-claw feet. On the floor we have a Persian rug, basically ruby red with beige and light blue accents. We have a damask-designed wallpaper in cream tones. Our draperies are cream colored over white curtains. Can you advise what color would be best for the seats of the dining chairs?*

A stripe is an excellent pattern for dining room chairs.

You should not be restricted to picking up one of the solid colors of beige, ruby red or blue for your chairs. Why not use one of the delightful stripes that are available? A small blue and gold stripe on a creamy vanilla background would be charming. If you are a bit daring, use a ruby red and vanilla stripe and braid the sides of the dining seats in gold.

Question: *Our living and dining rooms open into each other through a large arch. Both rooms have rough off-white plaster walls, beige wall-to-wall carpeting and parchment-colored draperies. The living room colors are aqua and gray. I want to get more color into both rooms by repainting the walls, and would also like to add color to the dining room by changing the draperies. Any suggestions?*

Orange is a happy dining room color.

How about painting all walls a pale apricot with fresh white semi-gloss enamel for the trim? For dining room draperies, how about a bright apricot, aqua blue, deep turquoise and white paisley pattern? Cover your dining room chair seats in bright, bright orange, and use orange throw pillows in the living room.

Question: *The wallpaper and draperies in the small dining room of our apartment are a coordinate of green and blue and white bamboo pattern. The floor is 12-inch squares of blue and white tiles laid on the diagonal. We want to paint our old table and chairs in a bright color. Does it have to be blue or green or white?*

Yellow, green and blue are adjacent colors on the color wheel. Use them for a well-blended dining room decorating scheme.

How about a bright sunny yellow for your furniture? The table can have a yellow laminated plastic top on a yellow lacquered base. Chairs might have yellow lacquered frames with yellow naugahyde upholstery. The lighting fixture over the table can also be sunny yellow. Put lots of green plants in earthenware pots on your window sill.

The Dining Room

Question: *We have just moved into our first apartment and are trying to figure out how to brighten up our dining area. The ceiling is white, the walls are honey beige, and the carpeting is beige. We are not allowed to change any of this. Our own draperies are white and our dining table and chairs are French provincial; the chairs are upholstered in beige, but could be done over. I am at my wit's end trying to figure out how to bring color into this room. Incidentally, the colors in the living room are mint green, lavender and beige.*

Dining rooms often offer less opportunity for color than other rooms of the home. Therefore, a multicolor print—strategically used—can be the answer.

Your dining room is certainly unappetizing the way it is! I'd begin by selecting a bright print to use for valances above your white draperies; a good color combination would be mint green, lavender, plum and sky blue. Trim the draperies with a plum border. Recover the chairs in a practical, sky blue fabric. As final spots of color, consider a lavender throw rug or two on top of your beige carpet.

Question: *Our dining room is done in red and pink. Our carpet is red tweed, the walls are light pink, and the ceiling is white. Our furniture is rustic French in pecan wood. I am about to pick out new draperies and dining room chair covers, which I want to be in the same material. What color do you suggest? I had thought of red and black.*

Garden chintz can sparkle in a dining room.

Don't use red and black for the draperies; that would kill your nice color scheme. First, paint all your trim a white. Then, use a fresh garden chintz for the draperies and chairs, perhaps one in red, pink, lime green, apricot and pecan on a white background. Drapery treatment could be stationary tiebacks with white sheer undercurtains. Use the same pattern on the chair seats, but have the fabric outline quilted first. Use either lime green or pale apricot placemats with pink napkins on your table.

Question: *I like my dining room's pale pink walls and draperies, and I also want to keep the poinsettia red seats on the chairs. But the room still needs something to make it more exciting. I'm considering an orange rug. Would that do it?*

The dining room is an ideal place to put a bright, bright rug.

By all means, use an orange rug in your dining room. Try to buy one with a bit of red in it. The dining room gets less traffic than other rooms, so is the perfect spot for light colored or bright colored rugs. Also, there are fewer opportunities for bringing color to a dining room than to other rooms, therefore, the rug should get special consideration. I would also buy some stock moldings at the lumberyard, paint them orange, and apply to your pale pink walls. For added interest, trim your pale pink draperies with red or orange braid or grosgrain ribbon.

The Kitchen

Thankfully, we are out of the clinical, laboratory decorating age with kitchens. Kitchens should be colorful, cheerful and an integral part of the entire home. Any period, style and color scheme is achievable today in kitchen decorating, thanks to cabinet designers, floor designers, fabric and wallpaper stylists, lighting planners and furniture designers. The designers have created their styles for manufacturers who show the products in stores and shops across the country.

Women spend lots of time in the kitchen: therefore, I advocate styling the kitchen in colors to suit the lady's fancy. Now, of course, there are lots and lots of male chefs. If you and your husband both enjoy the kitchen and preparing special dishes, kitchen planning and color selections should be discussed and decided by both partners.

I am all for casual meals served in the kitchen, and no kitchen should be without a table and chairs. If your space is truly limited, why not plan a mini-snack spot? The mini-snack spot can be a small table with a couple of chairs, or it can be a counter with a stool or two. Whether it's a table or counter, stools or chairs, use warm, cheerful colors for your kitchen eating area.

Ours is a great age for color in decorating products, and anyone who thinks a kitchen has to use dull neutral plastic laminates is completely off base. Look one day at all the brightly colored counter and cabinet laminates: shocking pink, apple green, sunshine yellow, avocado, ripe tangerine and just about every country garden color you can imagine. Many kitchen appliances now come with plastic laminated fronts and in wonderful fresh new colors to harmonize with your decor. Kitchen appliances seem to have followed the automobile industry in color styling. You can have a new-model range, refrigerator and dishwasher in the newest color—whatever color is now being dreamed up.

Let's choose a cheerful kitchen color scheme: lemon yellow, apple green, tangerine, white and a dash of chocolate brown. Now, let's see how we use these colors—and notice the variety and choices that make the kitchen your own. New cabinets can be a bright lemon yellow laminate, or existing cabinets can be painted a yellow enamel. Moldings or trim on the cabinets can be chocolate brown or white. If you decide to trim your cabinets with white, your kitchen appliances would be white;

chocolate brown moldings on the cabinets would call for brown appliances.

The counter tops can be a spicy tangerine laminate; they could also be a delicious apple green. Either one would be fine with the yellow cabinets. For wall decorating use a gay, wake-me-up print in a washable vinyl that incorporates the colors of your overall scheme. A floral print of yellow and orange marigolds with bright green leaves on a white background would be my choice. You can use the vinyl on your ceiling, too! Textures are playing an important part in decorating, and I would never hesitate to recommend a textured grass cloth vinyl for your kitchen walls and ceiling.

At the windows, you might use café curtains of a fabric that coordinates with your wall covering. They can be hung on wooden poles painted to match your counter tops. Or, you might prefer tangerine louvered shutters. I might also recommend shutters that have open panels: the shutter frames can be painted tangerine, and the panels filled with a white sheer fabric or with a fabric to match your wall covering.

For the floor of this kitchen, I'd select a vinyl—maybe white brick or yellow tiles that have a Spanish *olé!* feeling. Other choices within this color scheme would include yellow and white squares laid on the diagonal or bright yellow floor tiles with a chocolate brown feature strip.

A range hood is a large area of color in the kitchen and should therefore be chosen with care. So, if you have or plan to have a hood, and you want a great look over your range, choose stainless steel to coordinate with a stainless steel kitchen sink. To match counters, appliances, or trims, you can select a hood of copper or one of black wrought iron, or one covered with attractive mosaic tiles. You can have a hood with a facing of knotty pine or wormwood, or you can have a hood covered with a colorful plastic laminate. In the yellow, tangerine, green, white and chocolate brown kitchen we've just styled, the hood fascia can be covered with alternating stripes of bright yellow and white.

The country kitchen is a favorite of many people. It seems to me that we are returning to an age of real wood in the home. Wood seems to have that mellow, serene touch. If you are country-kitchen oriented, first pick your country. When selecting that special country think not only of colonial America. Think country French, think country Spanish, think country Austrian, think country Indian, think country Italian; think of all the countries you can, then decide which look appeals to you most and begin planning. Thanks to plastic laminates, you can now have the look

60

of an old paneled country kitchen with fresh new practical materials.

Early American kitchens can have knotty pine walls, braided rugs, rocking chairs, and lazy Susan tables. Country French kitchens may have painted wood walls, and natural wood floors. Country French kitchens often have tile counter surfaces, and rush-seat dining chairs with painted wood frames. I always enjoy seeing a painted French armoire in a chateau-designed room. The armoire is filled with colorful, fanciful plates, saucers, cups and, of course, spices.

Kitchens say spicy things to me, and a kitchen without bowls of fruits, hanging garlics or onions, is just not a place for full living enjoyment. Many people feel that a kitchen should be filled with cupboards and cabinets in which to hide everything, but why should a kitchen look institutional and unused? I feel that beautiful things should never be covered, thus I advocate the display of spices, plants, baskets, pots and pans, vegetables, fruits, dishes, apothecary and cookie jars in kitchen planning.

Fresh plants and herb plants always show personality in a kitchen. My wife and a number of people I know enjoy cooking, so there is hardly a time we don't have a pot of chives on our kitchen counter. The chives are used for salads and for seasoning in a host of other dishes. Our growing herbs and bottled spices give the kitchen a friendly look. I say "friendly" because I feel cooking for friends is the highest compliment you can pay them. If you are a spice nut, fill an armoire or a spice rack with all those flavors that will suit your fancy in many dishes.

I am all for cookbook corners in the kitchen. Perhaps you can find an old bookcase that you can paint or cover with self-adhesive vinyl that might fill the bill for a cookbook kitchen library. In a kitchen that I recently planned with a client, we removed the doors from two upper kitchen cabinets, painted the interiors the brightest color in the kitchen's scheme, and turned the space into the perfect spot for cookbook display.

Good kitchen lighting can help determine the mood of your decor. If you use fluorescent lighting anywhere in the kitchen, I recommend warm white deluxe tubes. Cold lighting can change food color. When appointing and accessorizing your kitchen, look at lighting fixtures carefully. There are brass fixtures for early American settings. There are wrought-iron lanterns and fixtures for that Mediterranean kitchen. There is not a kitchen around whose style cannot be enhanced with a great period or modern lighting fixture.

Does the kitchen have to relate in style and color to the dinette, dining room, family room, or living room? A self-contained kitchen does not have to relate, colorwise or stylewise, with any room in the house, if you so choose. Many people do relate rooms to one another; for example, it is very common to see a home with a colonial Williamsburg living room, dining room, kitchen and bedrooms. When people think modern, they generally translate their thinking into contemporary decor throughout all the rooms. The same is true with Mediterranean advocates and French, English and Italian enthusiasts. If you are a person of many moods, however, there is no reason why you can't have a Spanish-styled kitchen in a modern-furnished home, with some Spanish accessories in other rooms of the house.

Accessories play a most important part in good decorating, and the kitchen is a place where appointments can be used to advantage and in a casual way. There are a host of ways to sparkle up your kitchen table and counter tops. Porcelain pots in bright orange, sage green, yellow or some other vivid color would look handsome on your kitchen range. Straw baskets filled with fruits, vegetables or with growing plants always give dash to a room if they are hung from the ceiling or lined up on a window sill. Old chopping block tables are one of my favorite appointments for kitchens, as are old personality clocks and spice chests with drawers.

One of the most important areas of color in the kitchen is the top of the table. Decorate it with the colors and accessories you like. Are you fond of pink? Why not set your table or mini-snack spot with bright pink placemats of straw, cotton, linen, or plastic. Use bright orange napkins set into apple green napkin rings. White hobnail glasses would say a lot on the table, along with pink, orange, and green flowered plates. Coffee cups might be mandarin orange with white interiors and white handles. Your centerpiece could be a natural straw basket filled with daisies.

For an Italian meal in a country kitchen, why not lay a red and white checkered runner down the table? With royal blue napkins set into red napkin rings, your kitchen table will come alive with color and sunshine. Plain white dinner plates and clear stemmed tulip-shaped glasses filled with red wine would add sparkle. Centerpieces could be white candles set into old Chianti bottles, with red geraniums in natural clay pots.

Make the cooking and eating of food the fun it should be by putting lots of color into your kitchen and kitchen accessories. A good source of inspiration for color ideas for your kitchen would be a bowl of fruit or a basket of vegetables.

The Kitchen

Question: *I am remodeling my dinette and kitchen which are separated by an island. I have mahogany cabinets, white formica counter tops and avocado green appliances. There are two standard windows in the dinette area, and one window over the sink. Please recommend colors for walls, carpet and curtains.*

Green, brown and white geometric print carpeting is today's look for the kitchen.

So far you have avocado green, mahogany and white in your kitchen. Why not paint your walls sky blue and all the trim bright white semi-gloss enamel? For carpet, I strongly suggest you choose a patterned one. I have seen great geometric prints for kitchens. How about one in an avocado green, dark brown and white cane pattern? At your windows hang shutter frames painted bright white. In the inserts shirr an avocado green and sky blue checked fabric on small rods at the top and at the bottom. If possible, paint your dinette chairs a bright lemon yellow.

Question: *My husband and I are planning to redo our kitchen along the Americana line. We have metal cabinets which we must keep; the top sections are yellow and the bottoms are a brick color. We would like you to suggest the colors for the walls, floor and curtains.*

The most eye-catching feature in a colonial kitchen can be the color and texture of wood paneling.

A wood paneling for your kitchen walls would bring a touch of Early American into your kitchen. There are many types of easily installed wood-grain panels on the market in walnut, pecky cypress, wormwood, or whatever wood grain or stain you like. Louvered shutters painted yellow to match your top cabinets would be my suggestion as a window treatment. A vinyl brick would be a welcoming floor covering and would complement the color of your bottom cabinets. To carry out further the Early American look, hang an old lantern over your dining table and decorate your new wood walls with a collection of Americana memorabilia, such as old cookie cutters or wrought-iron trivets.

Question: *My kitchen looks very antiseptic, so I've been thinking of painting the cabinets. They are presently white, and so are the walls, counter tops and curtains. The floor is a red and white stripe. Should I change my curtains?*

Red and white kitchens with touches of black are popular.

Leave your counter tops white, but paint all your cabinets red and all baseboards black. Use black wrought-iron hardware on your bright red cabinets. Red and white striped café curtains, hung on white poles with black wooden rings would be a fun touch.

64

The Kitchen

Question: *We are about to redecorate our kitchen by staining the wooden cabinets, hanging new wallpaper, and maybe paneling half-way up one wall in the dinette area. We presently have light beige formica counter tops, coppertone appliances and a red brick floor. Could you advise us on color of wallpaper and cushions for black wrought-iron dinette chairs?*

Beware of too many dark colors in a kitchen.

First, I suggest you do not panel the wall in the dinette section of the kitchen. You already have the brick floor, coppertone appliances, and wooden cabinets so you are on the verge of a too somber kitchen. Go ahead and stain your cabinets; how about a rich French walnut color? Next, wallpaper all the wall space in kitchen and dinette area with a well-defined floral pattern of tangerine and bright blue with touches of avocado. Paint the ceiling white, and consider painting the black wrought-iron chairs white, too. Cover chair seats in alternating tangerine and blue textured vinyl.

Question: *The walls in our kitchen are pale yellow, and the counter tops and floor are mostly green with a little white running through. Our appliances are all white, and our furniture is pine. I have two windows that come together at a corner and one over the sink with a beautiful view of the mountains that I do not want to cover up too much. How shall I treat the windows?*

Bring the view from your kitchen window into your indoor color scheme.

Your yellow and green kitchen sounds most attractive, and I'm particularly glad that you do not want to close up your view of the mountains. I have always believed that people should bring the outdoors into their indoor decorating schemes. I would suggest bright yellow, pine green and sky blue printed curtains at your corner windows and a small ruffled valance of the print on the window over your sink. If you wish, you can install a roller shade under the valance. A yellow and white stripe contact vinyl adhered to the shade might be fun. The shade, of course, would be used only at night, when you want to close out the blackness. When the moon is shining on the mountain, I'd leave the shade up.

Question: *I'm planning to repaint my rather small kitchen. The floor covering is a neutral white beige with gold metallic sunbursts; the breakfast set is brown with a pecan wood grain top and gold beige chair covering on the seats; my counter top is beige. The cupboards have always been painted white, so a change would be welcome. What do you suggest for cupboards, walls and even the curtains?*

A kitchen needs much more color than beige and white.

Too many kitchens, even today, are predominantly white or beige, or a pallid institutional yellow or green. Your kitchen is no exception. How about a little color? Begin by choosing a snappy vinyl paper for all your wall area. Perhaps a trellis design in avocado green and lemon yellow on a bright white vinyl. Paint your cupboards a bright lemon yellow, and trim them in bright white. If there isn't any trim, put some on with molding you can buy at any lumberyard. Paint the molding bright white before you attach it. I might suggest that you hang white louvered shutters at your windows, with shiny brass pulls. Perhaps you have a place for a wicker plant stand. If so, fill it with green ferns.

Question: *My kitchen cabinets need refinishing, and I am not sure about the color. The ceiling is white, the wallpaper is white vinyl background with tangerine color snowflakes and a tiny gold-vein effect running all over, and the formica counter tops are a pale beige and tan pebble effect. All appliances are coppertone. I have used solid tangerine sheer curtains with white fringe at the window, which is accented by narrow black shutters. I have considered either harvest gold or antique red for the cabinets.*

Trim kitchen cabinets with painted 1-inch stock molding you can apply yourself.

I suggest you paint your cabinets a bright white. Purchase a 1-inch molding at the lumberyard and paint it a bright tangerine. Attach it to your cabinets to make a rectangular shape. Get rid of those black shutters at the window; they really don't serve any purpose other than to jar an otherwise pleasant color scheme.

66

Question: *We have remodeled our kitchen area, turning the old pantry into a breakfast room with a window. Now we would like to know what kind of furnishings and what colors to use in the new room. Our kitchen is colonial in style, with sunshine yellow cabinets, white appliances and Wedgwood blue on the little wall space. The floor of both kitchen and breakfast room is beige.*

Use the kitchen color scheme in a breakfast room.

Your kitchen has a happy color scheme which should be carried out in your breakfast room but in a different way. I'd look for a sunshine yellow, Wedgwood blue and white striped washable wall covering for your walls. Make sure there's a coordinated fabric for café curtains at the window. Cover the seat and back of an old deacon's bench with a blue and white floral colonial print fabric. Use the print on the seats of two captain's chairs. Accent your deacon's bench with some soft yellow cushions.

Question: *My kitchen is so drab. The walls are painted pale yellow, and the ceiling is white. I might add that wall space is limited. The counter tops are pale yellow marble on white. The cabinets are called bronze-glow birch. My avocado appliances increase the bland look. What do you suggest for walls, ceiling, window treatment and floor?*

Paint the kitchen ceiling the blue of God's sky.

Give your kitchen an immediate lift by painting the ceiling a lovely sky blue. Paint your walls a bright canary yellow and all the wood trim a bright white semigloss enamel. For the floor, how about an indoor-outdoor carpet in a cane pattern of white, yellow and chocolate brown? For the windows find an avocado brown, yellow and white plaid fabric.

Question: *I desperately need some help with my kitchen-dinette, the total area of which is quite small. I intend to frame the small windows with a valance and side panels in olive with a gold border. I will also make café curtains of a sheer gold material. My problem is the walls, which are now a drab white. The woodwork is oak.*

Wallpaper featuring oranges and lemons on green vines is a kitchen favorite.

Your kitchen needs a lift. Look for a vinyl wallpaper that has bright colored oranges and lemons on a lime green and emerald green vine against a white background. I have seen this wallpaper in several kitchens, and it is a joy to behold.

Question: *What color wallpaper and curtains would you use in my kitchen? The appliances are coppertone, the counter top tangerine, and the tile green.*

Coppertone appliances need a colorful background.

I would use a bright orange and emerald green floral on a white vinyl background as the wall covering and a melon and shocking pink plaid vinyl covering on the ceiling. Your kitchen curtains can be shocking pink trimmed with melon and white ball fringe. Lots of fresh greens in white china pots would be a further note of brightness for your kitchen decor.

Question: *I would like to purchase a butcher block for a kitchen table top but I'm not sure it will blend with the colors in my kitchen. Our walls are tiled in white with yellow and green tiles as a border. The counter tops are yellow, cabinets are white, and the floor is multicolor red, white, yellow, green, blue and black. If I do get a butcher block, what color should I paint the base of the table and the chairs? Also, I need to know what color and pattern to look for in some fabric for new café curtains I plan to make.*

The natural wood color of a butcher block fits any kitchen color scheme.

Go ahead and get your butcher block. It will look great as a table top. The table base can be a bright avocado green, and chairs can be bright lemon yellow. For the window, make café curtains of a lemon yellow, avocado green, red and blue plaid on a white background.

Question: *In my kitchen I have a red and white checkerboard floor, red counter tops and a white sink and stove. What color would you recommend for the walls and new curtains? I want the kitchen to look cozier, more traditional.*

A two-color checkerboard floor can be the base for either a traditional or modern kitchen.

You're lucky to have such a bright floor to begin with. What about painting your walls bright red with lots of white trim and ceiling? Café curtains can be a black and white floral print installed on a white wooden rod with white rings. These curtains will bring a more traditional look into your kitchen. Red, white and black is a sure-fire decorating scheme.

Question: *Our kitchen cabinets and center island are walnut with tomato red tops. The floor is also tomato red. I'd like a heavy, textured look on the walls but haven't found a suitable wallpaper. Do you have any suggestions as to color and pattern? Also, can those fake ceiling beams be used in a kitchen?*

Install ceiling beams with a walnut finish for a different look in the kitchen.

Yes, do put up two or three urethane ceiling beams spaced evenly on your ceiling. They will look especially good if your ceiling is finished in rough-textured white plaster. Your kitchen sounds so handsome as is! For your walls I would simply use a washable white vinyl with a rough-textured finish.

70

The Kitchen

Question: *My kitchen cabinets, stove island and hood are all bright yellow laminated plastic with white moldings. The walls are white. I want to replace the rather worn yellow counter tops and the yellow and white linoleum. What colors?*

Yellow, white and chocolate brown makes a happy good-morning color scheme for a kitchen.

I rather suspect you are a little tired of yellow, yellow, yellow. How about adding a deep contrasting color to your kitchen? Retile your floor with rich chocolate brown and snow-white 12-inch squares of vinyl laid on the diagonal. Your new counter tops can be a laminate in a rich brown walnut grain.

Question: *My dreary looking kitchen has light paneling, and the cabinets are also light natural wood. I do not like paneling. What color should I paint the cabinets? My appliances are white. The living room is next to the kitchen. It has red walls and black and white check curtains.*

Hang prints of luscious fruits or vegetables on kitchen walls.

Painted paneled walls are so good looking why not paint your walls and cabinets a bright white semigloss enamel? Paint the cabinet doors bright strawberry red. If you have a window, hang up a red and white striped roller shade. Fruit prints would be nice for pictures on the wall. How about strawberries, juicy blackberries and pink watermelons? They can be framed in red and white painted wooden frames. This kitchen scheme will work well with your living room.

Question: *My kitchen/family room is small. I have white floors, walls and appliances. The kitchen has walnut cabinets with gold trim, and a nondescript table with chairs. Do I treat the kitchen and family room as one? What wallpaper, window treatment and rug do you suggest? Should I paint the table and chairs?*

Unify a kitchen/family room with color.

To answer your first question: yes, do treat your family room and kitchen as one. Begin by choosing a color scheme besides just white. How about a white, lemon yellow and turquoise color scheme? Paint your walls bright yellow, and the ceiling a bright white. Kitchen chairs and table can be painted white. Put a bright turquoise and white patterned fabric on the chair seats, perhaps a zebra design. Use a narrow yellow, white and turquoise striped fabric at the windows, shirred on a wooden pole painted lemon yellow. For a rug, how about a cotton shag of turquoise, white and yellow squares in the family room? You could even make this rug yourself by collecting carpet samples and sewing them all together in an interesting arrangement.

Question: *We are going to install all new cabinets in our kitchen. I want them to be colorful, yet very easy to clean. The floor is a Betsy Ross red vinyl and the walls are white. What color do you suggest for the cabinets? Also, I need advice on window treatment. I don't like curtains in a kitchen; should I use thin white venetian blinds?*

Laminated plastic cabinets are practical and good looking when trimmed with moldings of a contrasting color.

A color scheme of red, white and blue would bring a star-spangled look to your kitchen. Cabinets can be laminated plastic in a rich Confederate blue with contrasting moldings of bright white. Clean white lacquered louvered shutters at the kitchen window would be easier to care for than venetian blinds and would have a warmer look.

Question: *I made my kitchen all white with black cabinets. Instead of being dramatic, it is quite dull. What should I change?*

A black and white kitchen needs a third color for warmth and interest.

Your kitchen will come alive if you cover your floor with toreador red vinyl or kitchen carpet and paint the doors of the upper cabinets the same red. Leave the lower cabinets black, and use bright brass hardware on all cabinets. Consider installing black beams on the ceiling to complete the Mediterranean look.

The Kitchen

Question: *I am building a kitchen at the front of the house. I plan to have a harvest gold range and refrigerator and walnut cabinets. I have a red cookie jar and avocado cannister set. What colors do you suggest for walls, flooring, counter top and draperies?*

White walls with walnut brown trim serve as a background for walnut cabinets.

For the flooring, my suggestion would be walnut brown and bright white 12-inch vinyl tile squares laid on the diagonal. Paint your walls bright white, and for all the trim use a walnut brown low-luster paint. Your counter tops can be a bright lime green satin finish plastic laminate. I suggest curtains of a lemon tree design. I have seen one that features bright yellow lemons on bark brown, lime green and avocado green on a white background. The fabric shirred on a lemon yellow painted pole would be fun.

Question: *I have a large kitchen/dining area with cream-color walls. The appliances are harvest gold, counter tops yellow and white, and cabinets a dark brown stain. The dining set has black metal legs with avocado green and yellow seats and backs. One wall of the dining area is covered by a large china cabinet of medium dark wood. Another wall has sliding doors that open onto a patio. I would like to paper the kitchen wall opposite the china cabinet, and use matching material for the window and sliding-glass doors. What could you suggest that would be bright and colorful? Chair cushions could be re-covered if it's advisable.*

Cover the kitchen walls and ceiling with a yellow, navy and white striped vinyl. Paint the inside of a china cabinet yellow.

My suggestion is to wallpaper every bit of wall space in your kitchen, not just the one wall you mentioned. How about a vinyl stripe covering in gold yellow, navy and white? Paint your chairs bright white, and reupholster them in shiny bright navy patent vinyl. Paint the inside of your china cabinet a bright canary yellow. It will look great with your new color scheme. For the curtains, how about a sheer cotton fabric of a subtle geometric weave in white to give you a fresh, open feeling, especially at your sliding doors?

Question: *My kitchen cabinets are oak with white tops. I have avocado appliances. My draperies in the dining area have a white background with an avocado, gold and tangerine design. The walls are tangerine. I would like to know what color you would recommend for new kitchen-dining area carpeting?*

Carry out a tangerine, avocado and off-white scheme in plaid carpeting.

Go tangerine, avocado and off-white—perhaps a plaid in these colors for your carpet. I have seen such a plaid, and it is sensational. It will look especially nice with your tangerine walls.

The Kitchen

Question: *I have only one question to ask: what color should I put on the floor of my kitchen? I like the walnut cabinets with their bright blue tops and the white walls, and I don't want to cover my pretty casement window. I only want to retile my floor some lovely, soft color.*

Try lavender with brown and bright blue for a dramatic kitchen color scheme.

You're right! You shouldn't change anything you like. I suggest a lovely soft lavender for your kitchen floor, and I'd buy an old artist's stool or two and paint them a bright purple to go with the kitchen floor.

Question: *We are about to choose the kitchen floor tile for our new home. Our appliances are harvest gold; the cabinets are fruitwood stained, and the counter tops are a white formica with specks of avocado. Since the room is narrow, we'd like a color of tile that will give the room a larger appearance.*

Horizontal stripes of white, avocado and yellow tiles can give a kitchen a wider look.

If your kitchen is narrow, what about installing alternating horizontal stripes of 12-inch vinyl tiles? First install a stripe of white tile, then a stripe of avocado tile, then a stripe of canary yellow tile. Continue alternating colors of tile until your floor is completely covered.

Question: *What do you suggest I do about drab plywood cabinets in my very small kitchen? Also, the walls should be repapered; what colors do you think would help cheer up the room?*

To unify and enlarge a small kitchen, paper cabinets and walls with the same colorful print.

I suggest you go ahead and wallpaper all the wall space, and do all the plywood cabinets, too! This will help unify your small kitchen. Make sure the wall covering is vinyl; it's so easy to clean and especially nice in a kitchen. Colors to look for in a print could be shocking mulberry, lemon yellow, bright white and avocado green.

Question: *I have remodeled my kitchen with cherry cabinets, copper-tone appliances, and straw yellow walls. I will be buying a new floor covering soon, as well as a new kitchen table and chairs. What colors would you recommend for these items?*

Brick vinyl floors are perfect for both colonial and contemporary kitchens.

Why not lay a brick vinyl floor in a herringbone pattern? Your kitchen table might be colonial in style with colonial captain's chairs.

The Kitchen

The finish of the table can be cherry. If you want to buy upholstered chairs, select those that have copper-color metal frames, with seats and backs upholstered in a colorful washable vinyl of sunny yellows and greens on a white background.

Question: *I have just purchased a new stove and refrigerator in avocado. I would like to repaint the yellow walls, and add curtains at the windows. What colors do you suggest?*

A lemon yellow, apricot and lettuce green color scheme enhances avocado kitchen appliances.

Freshen up your walls with a coat of lemon yellow paint and white semigloss enamel for the trim. Find a gay lemon yellow, apricot and lettuce green print on white background for the windows. I always like to see café curtains on painted or brass poles in a kitchen. Perhaps two sets would be nice: one to cover the upper part of the window and one to cover the lower part. If you have any breakfast stools or chairs in your kitchen, cover them in an apricot orange patent vinyl. What could be more practical and fun!

Question: *We are completely redoing our kitchen in the colonial style. I already have a colonial breakfast nook in maple; the upholstery, called oatmeal, is a dark brown and tan tweed. What color scheme would you suggest for a real colonial effect? I need new cabinets, appliances and accessories.*

White brick flooring in the kitchen can enhance the colonial look.

For a perky colonial kitchen, why not paint your cabinets a bright white with bright orange trim? Your new fixtures and appliances might be that rich copper-color enamel. Flooring should be a white brick vinyl tile. At the window hang bright white cotton frill curtains with bright orange cotton tiebacks. Perhaps an orange tree in an antique copper planter would look nice in your breakfast nook, if there is room.

79

Question: *What color wallpaper and curtains would you use in my kitchen? The appliances are turquoise, and the floor and counter top are beige.*

Paper a ceiling with flowers of many colors for a gay, colorful kitchen.

I would recommend a turquoise and white stripe wallpaper for your walls. On the ceiling I would use a flower print wallpaper, one that features orange, green, sky blue, yellow and bright red flowers on a white background. Your kitchen curtains can be bright yellow, installed on a turquoise blue wood pole. Kitchen table placemats and accessories can be any of the colors in the ceiling paper.

The Kitchen

Question: *My kitchen windows face north and east. The cabinets were white metal, but now have turned dark. The lower walls are yellow tile with black trim. The floor is white tile with tan and brown speckles. The counters are brown marble on white. At present the soffit is papered, but ordinary paper does not adhere to it. What do you suggest for my windows, walls above tile, and cabinets to make my kitchen a cheery place to work in?*

Try painting kitchen cabinets in alternating colors.

Your kitchen needs a lift. Why not paint your cabinets in alternating colors: pale yellow to match your tile, cheery cantaloupe and lettuce green. Cover your soffit with a melon and white carnival striped contact paper or wall vinyl. The wall above your tiles should be painted cantaloupe, the ceiling and trim can be white. At the kitchen windows hang curtains of a colorful print featuring yellows, melons, emerald greens and chocolate browns on a white background. Hang curtains on white wooden poles with white rings.

Question: *I would like to know what colors to use for walls, curtains, and tablecloth in our kitchen. The flooring is two shades of green. The cabinet top is white with green spots. I have dark paneling half-way up the walls and my appliances are coppertone and white.*

Color-key kitchen table accessories with the kitchen's colors.

I would suggest soft lemon yellow walls above your dark paneling. Paint your ceiling white and woodwork white semigloss enamel. On a rich emerald green pole with yellow rings, hang café curtains in a print that has lots of yellow flowers and green leaves on a white background. On your kitchen table, I'd use a rich copper color cloth and yellow napkins in emerald green napkin rings. White hobnail glasses and a centerpiece of fresh daisies would enhance the warmth of your kitchen and make it inviting.

Question: *My kitchen is long with a small window over a double sink and a large, double sliding-glass door. I would like red indoor-out-door carpeting (with a small black design in it) and small red and white flowered wallpaper for the upper half of the walls. The rest of the walls and ceiling would be an off-white. What colors, then, do you think I should select for draperies and curtains for the sliding-glass door and small window, and for new seats and backs for our dinette chairs?*

A red and white kitchen can be great, but don't overdo red. Add touches of other color.

You sound pretty much organized on your kitchen color scheme. It will look great! I might make a few suggestions. If you plan to paper only the top half of the wall, be sure to put up a dado to break the transition from paint to wallpaper. Try to find a paper that has a little green and black in it in addition to the red and white. You are getting too much red. Don't paint your walls and ceiling off-white. Paint them bright, clean white semigloss enamel. As for your sliding-glass door, leave it alone. If you want privacy, hang bright white cotton sheer fabric curtains from the top of your door. Make them very full with a shirred heading. For your other window, I suggest you make a shade from your wallpaper. Seats and backs of your dinette chairs can be a bright red patent vinyl.

Question: *The walls of my kitchen are newly paneled in white, with a white brick vinyl tile floor, birch cabinets and woodwork and white appliances. The counter tops and dinette set are beige and white. What color could be used at the window or elsewhere?*

White and beige is a boring kitchen color scheme. Add shocking pink and lemon yellow to make it come alive.

Begin by bringing color into your kitchen. So far, you have white and beige—what a bore. How about reupholstering your dinette chair seats in shocking pink? If at all possible, repaint your paneled walls bright lemon yellow, with white semigloss enamel for the trim. Find a shocking pink, lemon yellow and white cotton fabric for curtains at the window. Go wild when it comes to accessories, perhaps a mod canister set in shades of pink, purple and yellow. How about some baskets filled with vibrant green ivy and ferns? Paint the baskets yellow, shocking pink and bright white.

83

The Bedroom

There are so many rooms called bedrooms. Often, the only thing they have in common is that someone sleeps in them. From the crib in the nursery to the king-size bed in the master bedroom, from the teenager listening to records to the grandmother relaxing on her chaise—there is an endless variety to the styles and uses for the bedroom.

There are as many ways to decorate bedrooms as there are people who occupy them. The bedroom is a very personal room, and you want it to be your personal background, reflecting *you*. The bedroom is the first room you see each day. Do you want it to sing you awake with bright cheer? Then you'll go for sunny, country garden colors. Do you retreat to your bedroom during the day to put your feet up and relax? Perhaps you want the feeling of serenity and softness in your room. You may choose cool colors adjacent to each other on the color wheel.

Whatever the mood or feeling you wish to create, color is the tool. Color is also a very personal preference so each member of the family should occupy a room that pleases him or her in terms of color. Children should always be consulted about color when their rooms are being decorated. Certainly a teenager should take part in the execution as well as the planning of his room.

Most youngsters today want studio-bedrooms in which to entertain and study by day, and sleep at night. They want their favorite colors in their rooms, usually vivid, contrasting ones. Before planning and decorating that room, consult your child; use his choice of colors—even if *you* don't care for them. I think you will find that the youngster will take a lot of interest in his room, particularly in keeping it clean and neat, if the room reflects his color preferences. A child's room is fun to decorate, but it must be fun for the child as well as the parent.

You can't very well consult your new or expected baby about his choice of colors. In this case, you must rely on your instincts as a parent. You know babies respond to bright, primary colors; you want your baby to be surrounded by warmth and cheerfulness. Armed with your healthy intuition, your knowledge of babies in general, and your love for your own baby in particular, you can come up with a color scheme for the

85

nursery that will be charming and gay. And, if you are unafraid of color, it will also be different, unusual and fun.

You may be starting from scratch with an empty bedroom and a fat purse or working with old furniture and a limited budget. You may be planning a guest room or a seating arrangement in a corner of a master bedroom. Whatever kind of bedroom you are working toward, your success will be measured by how effectively you use color.

What are the major color areas in the bedroom? As in any other room, you can begin with walls, floor and ceiling. Then there are the colors and/or wood tones of your furniture, the upholstery of the chair or chaise, the draperies or curtains. Unique to the bedroom, however, is the bed with its spread, pillows and headboard. The colors of the accessories—lamps, pictures and dressing table appointments—must be chosen as carefully as though they were to be displayed in your living room. Changing any one of these color areas can change the mood or feel of your room.

Unless you are starting from scratch, you must decide how many color areas in your bedroom you can or should change, how much of your present color you must, or wish to, keep. Perhaps painting or papering the walls is all that is needed to transform your room. New spreads, draperies or carpet? Does your furniture need refinishing or repainting? Whatever else your redecorating involves, it must involve color, and bedroom color schemes should suit the personality of the person or persons occupying the bedroom.

Too often, the master bedroom is planned around the woman's personality only. This is wrong! I believe that a woman should plan the color scheme of her bedroom *with* her husband as a consultant. Men are as interested in color as women are.

If a woman wants a pink bedroom with bright rose accents, she should have it. Pink is a very flattering color to women, and it doesn't strip a man of his masculinity. It oftentimes enhances it. Pink and red in a master bedroom can satisfy both occupants.

Green is another favorite color for the bedroom. But beware of the pale, institutional green that is so dull and dreary. It is a bad bedroom color, because it pales the skin color. But bright green as part of a total color scheme can be lovely. Picture a bright yellow, white, and emerald green master bedroom scheme, for instance.

There are many beige and gold bedrooms in America. I believe beige bedrooms can be soft and flattering, but the bland decorating days are gone. To be successful, the furnishings of a beige room must be of a highly distinctive nature. Walls should be hung with special, colorful art works; accessories and table appointments must be bright and colorful.

Certainly the finish and style of furniture must be taken into account when redecorating a bedroom. But I am against matching bedroom suites. You should mix the furniture's wood finishes and paints, and treat them as part of the color scheme. Play up the wood tones in your bedroom set with color.

If your bedroom and bathroom adjoin each other, why not use the same color on your bathroom walls as is on your bedroom walls, and the shower curtain could be the same fabric or color as your bedspread and draperies.

Your bed is usually the focal point of the room. I usually like a multi-color print on the bed, a print that combines the colors in the room's total scheme. And most bedspreads should be quilted for that soft, warm look. When your spread is removed from the bed, the bed linens and blankets should blend into the room's color scheme. You will have no difficulty in finding sheets, pillowcases and blankets to match or complement any color in your room.

Question: *My bedroom has purple carpeting and pink walls. My mother is letting me decorate the rest of the room any way I want. What colors should I look for in a bedspread and curtains, and also, what color for new furniture which will last me through college?*

Wicker is a good choice for bedroom furniture.

Your furniture can be white with a pink trim or pink with white trim. Wicker furniture would be a good choice. A bright pink, purple and mint green print on a white background would be great for curtains under a purple swag valance lined in mint green. Use the print for your bedspread, with a mint green flounce.

Question: *I have a scarlet love seat in my bedroom, as well as a rocker and other antique furniture. What colors do you suggest for carpet, walls and bedspread? My draperies are white.*

Pink and white walls and red carpeting in a bedroom provide a setting for antiques.

Bright red would be my choice for carpeting. Walls might be covered in a pink and white ticking or with a small pink and white flowered paper. The bedspread should be white trimmed in red; colorful pink, red and white throw pillows on your bed would further enhance the overall decor.

Question: *Our bedroom rug is medium red, the walls are white, and our furniture is mahogany. What colors can be used for bedspreads, curtains and pillows? I don't like greens.*

Try a red, white and lemon yellow decorating scheme in a bedroom.

One of the combinations I particularly like is red, white, and lemon yellow. Why not use ruffled, solid lemon yellow bed skirts, with the bedspread in a red-on-white print with a touch of gold in the design. Bed pillows should be mixed—white, yellow, red. The curtains can be one of the many organdy crisscross white varieties.

88

The Bedroom

Question: *We are about to redecorate our bedroom by buying a new bedspread and curtains. The walls are white, and we'd like to keep them that way. We have bright green wall-to-wall carpeting, and a chaise lounge also in bright green. Please help us with our purchases. We've been considering a canopy at the head of the bed for a different look.*

Use those wake-up colors—red and green—in your bedroom.

Find a print of bright cherry red flowers, green leaves and brown stems on a white background. Use this for a quilted bedspread, canopy and a Roman shade at your window. Line the bed canopy in a green and white trellis design. For a special note, use a red hassock or bench at the foot of the bed and a red throw pillow on the chaise lounge. A potful of geraniums would be a marvelous accent, too.

Question: *When I ask my little girl what colors she wants in her room, she names five or six flower colors. Can that many colors be used in one room?*

Use a multitude of colors in a little girl's bedroom. She'll love it!

Pink, yellow, red, purple, green and blue—all in one room. They work together and give a summertime look to a young girl's bedroom. For instance, walls can be covered in a modern yellow, pink and purple floral pattern on a white background. A daybed can be upholstered in a pink and red check, with window café curtains to match. Lots of colorful purple, yellow and green pillows can be accents for the daybed. A chair can be painted yellow, and its seat can be upholstered in brilliant red patent vinyl. Use a yellow washable cotton area rug on the floor near the bed.

The Bedroom

Question: *I want to redecorate our teenage son's room. The furniture is tawny maple and the rug is light gray. What colors would you suggest for the bedspread, draperies, walls and lampshades?*

Paint bedroom closet interiors a bright color for a surprise opening.

A gray rug is rather dull for a youngster's bedroom. To make it less noticeable, I would suggest painting all the walls bright red; paint the trim, doors and ceiling white. Paint the interior closet walls a bright royal blue with white shelves and hanging pole. Buy a royal blue and white checkered spread for the bed. Use the same fabric for café curtains hung on a white pole with white wooden rings. A grouping of Confederate prints on the walls, matted with wide borders, framed in royal blue or silver would add a good touch. A silvered lamp with a bright white shade would be my choice for the lamp. Assorted red, white and blue corduroy pillows on the bed would coordinate with the overall decorating scheme.

Question: *My bedroom carpeting is dark avocado, the king-size bed has a red velvet headboard, and the bedroom chair is red velvet. I realize now that red was the wrong color to choose for the headboard. The wallpaper in this room has a neutral background with a gold figure here and there. I want to redo the headboard, and get a new spread and draperies, but am unable to decide what would be the best colors.*

A headboard upholstered in the same fabric as the bedspread makes a bedroom look extra-rich and bright.

If at all possible, reupholster your headboard in the same fabric as the bedspread. How about a lettuce green and lemon yellow floral print on a neutral background (the same as the wallpaper) for the spread? My choice for throw pillows would be lettuce green piped in red and lemon yellow piped in red. Find the same neutral background color in a linen fabric for your draperies, and line them in lettuce green.

Question: *We are redecorating a small bedroom for our nine-year-old boy. If we were to panel or wallpaper the room, would it appear smaller? I would like suggestions for carpeting, windows and for painted furniture.*

Yellow and blue vinyl tiles laid in stripes can make a small bedroom look larger.

I would not recommend panels for the walls. Use a dado of a soft fruitwood if you like. Above the dado use vinyl washable wall covering in a bright plaid of yellow, green, blue and red on a white background. Paint doors, windows and ceiling white. Hang bright yellow louvered shutters at the window. For the floor, lay 12-inch vinyl tiles across the room in alternating stripes of yellow and blue to give the room a wider look. I would recommend royal blue furniture with white drawer pulls. Paint the interiors of the drawers a fire engine red. For bedspread and bolsters, I'd use red corduroy.

Question: *My teenage daughter insists on red shag carpeting in her bedroom. Her furniture is pecan and she has a black rocker. Aside from this, we will be starting from scratch. Can you offer some suggestions about the color of the bedspread, draperies and walls?*

Bright plaids are young and gay in a teenager's bedroom.

Teenager's rooms are such fun to decorate. If your daughter likes red, by all means use coral red cotton shag carpeting. Why not paint the walls a mauve pink with white semigloss enamel for the trim and ceiling? For the bedspread, I suggest a mauve pink, cantaloupe orange, coral red and white plaid cotton quilted bedspread, and perhaps the same fabric for draperies. Tie back the draperies with big bows made of the same fabric, and shirr them on to a cantaloupe orange painted pole. Paint a wicker headboard lime green. Put mauve pink and lime green throw pillows on the bed. A little lime green cushion on the black rocker would be great. What a fresh, cheerful room for a young girl!

Question: *My bedroom is quite modern; a purple lacquered bed with bare canopy, white lacquered night tables, black lacquered rocker with cane back and orchid shag carpeting. What colors would you recommend for the bedspread and walls?*

Deep purple, orchid and sky blue bring a bedroom up to date.

Paint your walls a soft sky blue with white ceiling and trim. For the bedspread, I'd find an exciting geometric print featuring plum, blue and canary yellow on a white background. Every room needs an unexpected touch. For your bedroom, I'd recommend a shocking red modern painting over the bed.

Question: *What would be good colors in a north-facing bedroom? We are planning to redecorate ours, and want it to appear light, though in reality the room receives no direct sunlight.*

North-facing bedrooms should have sunshine colors in the fabrics and on the walls.

In your north bedroom why not use nature's decorating scheme! Consider sky blue walls and a grass green carpet on the floor. Hang a country garden floral print at your windows, one that features rose reds, delphinium blues, emerald greens and buttercup yellows on a white background. Use the print for your bedspread over a buttercup yellow bed skirt. The slipper chair or chaise upholstery color can be grass green. The furniture can be dark brown walnut. Lamps can be a bright white.

Question: *I have a crewel-pattern drapery in my bedroom over sheer curtains. I would like to use a wallpaper on the walls but do not know what color or pattern would blend well with the draperies. The predominate color of the draperies is Indian red; there are also oranges and corals in the fabric. My bedspread is royal blue.*

Crewel patterns give bedrooms a special touch.

To go with your crewel draperies, I would suggest a pale orange and champagne beige flamestitch design for the wallpaper. Also, try to find a wallpaper that has a coordinating fabric so you can have pillows on your royal blue bedspread to match the wallpaper. Another throw pillow for the bed could be covered in a royal blue and Indian red stripe.

Question: *We are planning to redecorate our bedroom. We have red carpet and white provincial furniture. What colors would you recommend for the walls, draperies, and curtains?*

Match a bed's dust ruffle to bright print draperies.

I love red in the bedroom. Why not use a bright red, emerald green, and sky blue floral drapery fabric at your windows, under sky blue valances lined in bright red. White nylon would be my suggestion for undercurtains. Use a dust ruffle on your bed to match the drapery, and a sky blue quilted bedspread. Throw pillows on your bed can be of the print also. For accessories, I'd use white lamps with white translucent shades.

Question: *Our bedroom has gray blue walls, a white ceiling and woodwork and gray carpet. We would appreciate some suggestions about bedspread colors and accents. The furniture is maple. The night table lamps are white hobnail. The room has a southwestern exposure.*

Too much gray makes a bedroom depressing. Use watermelon to add cheer.

You have too much gray in your bedroom. How about a watermelon red quilted throw-style coverlet for the top of your bed and a sunny yellow, sky blue, watermelon red and grass green garden cotton print on a white background for the gathered dust ruffle? Be sure to buy enough of the garden print fabric to make pleated valances for your draperies. Throw pillows can be sunny yellow, sky blue and grass green.

Question: *Something is wrong with our master bedroom, but I don't know what. It has white walls, and avocado draperies, bedspread and throw rug. On the bed we have pink pillows to match a painting hung over the headboard. There is one gold upholstered chair. Please tell me what is wrong or what colors need changing.*

A bedroom planned only with solid colors is generally boring. Try some print fabrics for a fresh start.

Everything in your bedroom is a solid color. What about a pink and green print slipcover for your gold chair? Use the print for valances over your avocado draperies and for a bed dust ruffle. You might even consider a pink and white striped ticking for your headboard wall. A print and a stripe work very well together in all decorating schemes. Be sure to use a gold pillow or two—along with the pink pillows—on your avocado spread.

95

Question: *My bedroom is nearly all beige: beige walls, beige draper-ies over white sheer casement curtains, a beige area rug with a green vine entwined border. The bed is brass, and the rest of the furniture is walnut. I have been using a white bedspread which I want to change. What color bedspread should I get? What else can I do to bring some life into the room for not much money?*

A strictly beige and brown bedroom is unhappily decorated.

Your room can be transformed with just two changes. Paint the walls a clean cantaloupe, and cover your bed with a quilted bedspread of bright oranges, greens and yellows on a white background. Either change by itself would not be sufficient, but both will give you a lovely room.

The Bedroom

Question: *We want to create a guest room in our attic. It's a small area, with sloping ceiling and a window at one end. We need your advice on the color of everything—from floor to ceiling, from bedspread to curtains.*

Make your guest room say welcome with soft blue, azalea pink and white.

For a warm glow, color your guest room in soft simple colors. Put down white vinyl flooring. Paint the window wall white, and install white shutters and beneath the window, a white lacquered shelf. Paint the other walls and the ceiling azalea pink. Cover the bed in a blue fabric with thin white crisscrossing lines to give a plaid effect. On a white lacquered night table place a lamp with a pottery base and a blue shade, perhaps in the bedspread's fabric. Lots of green plants on the window shelf would make your guests feel at home.

Question: *I would like to know what colors to look for in a bed-spread and draperies for our master bedroom. The walls are painted bone white, the furniture is dark mahogany and the wall-to-wall carpeting is antique gold.*

Solid color draperies in a bedroom can be made distinctive by trimming with the bedspread print.

Your bedroom needs life! I would suggest a gold, delphinium blue, melon and emerald green floral on a white background for your bed-spread, over a soft melon bedskirt. Please be certain the bedspread is quilted for a puffy comfortable look. For draperies I would suggest using the solid melon trimmed with a 12-inch-wide panel of the print. Use swag-and-jabot valances made of the print and lined in gold.

Question: *We have a bedroom paneled in cherry with an end wall papered in a paisley print of tomato red, French blue and chocolate brown. My 16-year-old daughter must now use this room as her bed-room. I feel it is too masculine, and would like any suggestions you may have for the shutters, louvered closet doors and a built-in chest of drawers; also curtains, bedspread and floor covering. She would like the room to be as much a gathering place for her friends as a bedroom.*

Pick up paisley colors in a geometric print. Yes, two prints live well to-gether.

The fabric for the bed might be a snappy geometric pattern in these colors: lemon yellow, French blue, and chocolate brown. Throw pillows can be lemon yellow, tomato red, melon orange, navy blue, and lime green. These colors will go great with that paisley-papered wall. Your built-in chest might be painted a lemon yellow, and if the knobs are made of wood, paint them a tomato red. Find a lemon yellow and French blue shag carpet. If there is room, put a tomato red lacquered Parsons table in front of the bed. It might be 30-inches square and coffee table height. The whole gang can sit on the floor around the table for snacks and talk.

98

Question: *We are converting a child's bedroom into a guest room (the child having grown up). The bed sits in an alcove. What colors do you suggest for the walls, bedspread and rug? I want a really different look, something exotic!*

Try the Moroccan look for a dazzling guest room.

An orchid and blueberry paisley print on the walls would be really different; use the same print in a coordinated fabric for your bedspread. Hang a Moroccan brass lantern over the bed. An old filigree chair painted brassy yellow would be effective. Paint an old end table brassy yellow, too. Put a pale blue rug on the floor, and on the bed, accent pillows in blue-on-blue and red-on-blue.

Question: *What color should we paint our bedroom walls which are presently white? The carpet is green, and the bedspread and draperies are a blue and green floral print on white. I am also interested in a third color for accent. We have a chair by a glass-top table we could paint.*

Accent colors can change a merely "nice" bedroom into a vibrant one.

Paint your walls a sky blue to tie the major colors together in your bedroom. Woodwork and ceiling should be bright white. Then for an accent color, paint your chair red, and cushion it in the same blue as your walls. Small accessories, such as ashtrays, could be yellow.

The Bedroom

Question: *I'm 13-years-old, and I wish there was a way I could perk up my bedroom. The furniture is white with gold trim. The bed's canopy and spread are a pattern of blue flowers and green leaves. The rug has flowers in many colors. I just painted an extra large abstract picture which I want to hang. Please tell me how to frame it. Also, could you give me some ideas for inexpensive curtains? I want a mixture of the feminine look with the modern.*

Paint wooden spools and string them up for curtains in a girl's room.

You sound very girlish, which is what girls should be; yet the picture you painted sounds as if you are right in tune with today. Strip frame your painting in white lacquer or silver. For your windows, why not make a curtain out of wooden thread spools. Collect as many spools as you can and paint the spools blue and white and green. The blue and green should be the same colors as the leaves and flowers in your spread and canopy. String the spools by alternating the colors, and hang the strings of spools from your curtain rod. Another idea would be to paint a new picture on your window shade. I know many young people who paint designs and pictures on their window shades. Some even cover their shades with exciting printed or striped contact paper.

Question: *I am in the process of redecorating a rather drab attic bedroom. The walls are soft white, the rug antique gold, and the chest of drawers has a white finish. What colors would you suggest for the bedspread, draperies and chair cover?*

Lots of white and bright colors can turn an attic area into a lively liveable bedroom.

Attic rooms are usually small and closed in, with little light. If this is the case, I would suggest white nylon curtains at the window, something filmy to let in lots of light. A shirred dust ruffle on the bed might be white nylon also. The bedspread can be gold, pink, white and green print, outline-quilted to pattern. A comfortable chair in the room should be covered in the quilted print. Throw pillows on the bed can be pink and white.

101

Question: *I would appreciate color suggestions for inexpensive curtains and rug in a baby's nursery. I have already painted the walls white and have hung an 18-inch border of nursery paper at the ceiling. The paper is colored in peachy orange, brown and beige.*

Brightly colored construction paper makes a valance for the windows in a nursery.

For your windows, I'd make a paper valance. First, accordion-pleat yellow, white and orange construction paper. After pleating the sheets of paper, put the sheets—alternating the colors—through a standard, adjustable curtain rod, and hang the new paper valances at your windows. A white window shade striped with yellow and orange strips of contact vinyl would further enhance the overall look. A bright orange cotton rug on the floor would be handsome, one with a beige or yellow border.

Question: *I have blue green carpeting in my boy's bedroom; the walls are the light green shade in the carpeting. The draperies are a blue green blend. The furniture is olive green. I would like your help in selecting a bedspread.*

The hunter's colors of red and green are sure-fire decorating magic in a boy's room.

I can see that your boy's room is overly green. Go solid red, red, red for the bedspread, or consider a red and white hounds-tooth check. A red and white geometric print or a red and white flamestitch would be a good wall accent. A night-table lamp could also be red.

Question: *I have a blond bedroom set with a four-poster bed. What color should I paint the walls? What colors should I use for bedspread and draperies?*

Blond furniture can sparkle in bedrooms when the walls are painted a medium or deep-tone shade.

I like blond furniture in rooms that have walls painted a medium to deep tone. You could paint your bedroom walls a clear Wedgwood blue with sparkling white trim. Alternatives would be apple green with white or peony pink with white. Use a white Martha Washington spread and lots of colored pillows on your four-poster bed. Windows can be treated with crisscross organdy curtains or with white cotton draw curtains of a solid color vertical stripe. The color of the stripe should match the wall color.

Question: *My 18-year-old son wants me to redo his room in black, white and some contrasting color for an ultramodern look. Is it permissible to have walls painted black? What about draperies and curtains?*

Black and white bedrooms can be dramatic if a third color is selected carefully.

An 18-year-old is a young man of a very responsible age, and I would certainly let him plan his own room. If he likes black, why don't you paint the doors in the room black? The walls and ceiling should be white. Use black louvered shutters at the window, and a black rug on the floor. Paint all the furniture a true fire engine red, and use a black and white plaid as the bedspread. The closet interior should be painted fire engine red.

Question: *I want to redecorate my bedroom around a beautiful quilt woven of lavender and purple with light touches of green. My carpeting is beige. I had thought of using lavender for draperies and dust ruffle and light violet for the walls. Do you have any other suggestions?*

Trim white draperies with velvet ribbon borders to coordinate a bedroom's colors.

For a sharp contrast and more impact, you might consider lavender for the walls, with white draperies. Trim the draperies with velvet ribbon borders of purple, lavender and light violet. I like the lavender idea for the bed skirt. Hanging white wicker baskets filled with pretty greens could add a lot to your room, as would a row of potted African violets on the window sill.

103

Question: *I am 16 years old, and I need help to pep up my room. I have to keep the cherry red carpeting, and I like my white furniture. What should I do with my canopy bed, walls, and the window?*

Use the same print on walls, ceiling, windows and bed to achieve an exciting bedroom for a young lady.

Splash the same bright, fresh print over walls, ceiling, bed and window for a different, dazzling look. In your case I'd choose a pink, lavender and lipstick red flowered pattern on a white background. Paper walls and ceiling with the print. Use a coordinated fabric for café curtains, and have it quilted for a spread. Your bed canopy should be white with a red ball fringe border.

104

The Bedroom

Question: *The window wall of my bedroom is all built-in cabinets except for the window and window seat. The cabinets are painted pink semigloss enamel; the rest of the walls are white. My carpeting is emerald green. I want a new bedspread and new window treatment—something besides curtains. What do you suggest? Also, my bed has a high, flat headboard which I'm thinking of painting pink. Please tell me if that would be right.*

Use the same print fabric for window seat, shade and bed to coordinate the colors in a bedroom.

Your pink and green room needs a colorful pink, blue, emerald green and red floral print on a white background to tie the room together. Use the print on a Roman shade at your window and on window seat cushions. The print should be your bedspread, and instead of painting your headboard, cover it with the print for a more coordinated look. Use throw pillows of blue and green on your window seat.

Question: *We are going to turn a basement room into a sleeping-study room for our 18-year-old son, who lost his bedroom to a grandparent. At present the basement room is paneled in light wood. Do you have any ideas for decorating and furnishing? There is one small window.*

Cover a basement bedroom window with a bright shade or shutters.

Since the basement is already paneled in light wood, you might find a handsome plaid carpet in the rich tones of chocolate brown and melon orange on an oatmeal color background. For the one small window take an ordinary white window shade and, with an acrylic-base paint, paint stripes of chocolate brown and melon orange, or hang bright melon orange louvered shutters at the window. You might use corduroy for the bedspread, and choose a bright cheerful melon orange. Place some fake fur throw pillows on the bed for fun and comfort.

Question: *I plan to redecorate a den to make it into a small bedroom. Two walls are paneled in pine and two are painted white. The furniture is French provincial in a pickled pine. I have a handmade quilt that I will use for the bedspread; the quilt has a lot of color in the design, including pink, and the background is yellow. What colors do you suggest for carpet and draperies? Should I paint the paneled walls?*

Paneled walls in a bedroom often look best painted.

By all means, paint the paneled walls white. Your handmade quilt sounds terrific. With it, why not use a white cotton dust ruffle trimmed at the bottom with a braid in pink, yellow and green? My suggestion for your carpet is a strawberry pink shag. Draperies can be a paisley pattern in shades of strawberry pink, sunshine yellow and grass green. You might install the draperies on a strawberry pink painted wooden pole with strawberry pink wooden rings.

The Bedroom

Question: *My teenage son wants a studio-type bedroom with a tailored look. We have a studio couch to start with, which needs to be slipcovered. We have a blue and green tweed area rug, and a bookcase. The walls are painted white. What colors would you choose for couch and curtains?*

Use the two very cool colors of blue and green in a boy's studio bedroom.

A bold apple green and blue plaid on a white background would be my selection for your studio couch cover, bolsters and café curtains. I'd find some old furniture—perhaps a chest or a captain's chair, depending on what you need—and paint it bright apple green. Accent the setting with some spicy colors like canary yellow and paprika orange.

Question: *My traditional bedroom has walnut furniture, lemon yellow carpeting and white walls. I like soft, mellow colors, but I don't want a dull, subdued room. What do you suggest for new draperies, bedspread and chair coverings? One chair is a lounge chair, the other is a pull-up side chair.*

Yellow with cantaloupe and apricot would be a happy winner in a traditionally furnished bedroom.

Try to find a floral print consisting of cantaloupe, tangerine and lavender on a summertime yellow background. Hang the print as draperies under a creamy apricot velvet swag-and-jabot valance. Use the apricot velvet as the upholstery on your lounge chair. The print fabric can be quilted for the bedspread, and the seat of the pull-up side chair can be covered in the print, too.

Question: *There is a gray blue, watered blue and gold fleck wallpaper on the walls in our teenage boy's bedroom. Please give me color ideas for the bedspread and throw rugs.*

Make pillows of flags for a boy's bedroom.

Your son's room needs brightening up. I would suggest a rich royal blue rug on the floor, with a royal blue and fire engine red bedspread. Curtains at the windows can be Confederate red café style on a rich royal blue or brass rod. What about making a couple of stars and stripes pillows for the bed? There are a number of different flaglike design fabrics on the market that are both young and inexpensive. (Do not use real flags!) Discuss the decorating plans with your son before you do anything. He might prefer an emerald green and yellow scheme for the room, or a chocolate brown and orange look. Both these combinations would also work with your wallpaper.

Question: *In changing from a "baby room" to a "little girl room," we must keep red plush carpeting. Could we have pink walls? What would you suggest for window treatment for a single window? We have a low-poster bed which we are refinishing in white. We also have a white chest and rocker. What about a swag above the bed, and what would be appropriate for bed covering?*

Curtain the wall section behind a bed to match the dust ruffle for a striking look.

To begin with, pink is fine for your walls. Use a petal pink with white woodwork and ceiling. Hang white crisscross ruffled organdy curtains at the window over a window shade made of a pink, green and white flowered print. Use the print, quilted, for the bedspread. I'd forget about a swag valance over the bed. If you want a drapery look why not curtain the wall section behind the bed with shocking pink? Use the same shocking pink fabric for a skirt on the bed. If you paint the bed white consider trimming it in brilliant red!

109

Question: *In redecorating my bedroom, I am starting from scratch except for the bedroom set which is modern and gray. Please tell me whether I should paint it or antique it, and what color. Also, I need your advice about the rest of the room.*

Painting old bedroom furniture can save hundreds of dollars, yet give a room a new, bright look.

Why not paint your furniture spanking white lacquer and change the hardware to royal blue pulls? Go today-modern with royal blue walls and lots of white trim. Hang a royal blue-on-white geometric print drapery at your windows on rich brass poles. For your bedside tables buy some inexpensive brass lamps with white shades. The bedspread can be white with a canary yellow bed flounce. Different size pillows of yellows and whites can be tossed on your bed. Carpet your room in salmon pink or eclipse yellow.

Question: *Our daughter, aged 17, is redoing her room. The walls and ceiling slope. Walls, ceiling and woodwork are all white. The floor is hardwood, and the furniture, including an antique deacon's bench, is oak. We need new curtains for the dormer window and a new bedspread. What could you suggest?*

Patchwork quilts give a colonial bedroom the multicolor look.

Your daughter seems to like antiques and the colonial look. Perhaps she would like one of those great colorful patchwork quilt bedspreads of many colors—white, reds, greens, yellows, blues and oranges. Window curtains should pick up the most vibrant color in the quilt spread, perhaps a shocking red or a brilliant royal blue.

Question: *We want to panel our daughter's bedroom. What would you suggest for panel color and other colors to use?*

White wormwood paneling is light and bright in a bedroom.

First, visit a local carpentry shop or hardware store to see the many different kinds of paneling on the market. Take your daughter with you, and ask her which paneling appeals to her most. I personally

110

like a wormwood paneled room, painted flat white, because with it you can use any of a million different decorating schemes. Consider Siamese pink carpeting with bright canary yellow curtains. The bedspread could be a Siamese pink, canary yellow, and mandarin orange Indian print. Yellow lacquered wicker furniture trimmed in Siamese pink would be exciting, along with mandarin orange toss pillows on the bed.

Question: *I want to redecorate our seven- and 11-year-old sons' bedroom. The room is on the southwest corner of the house. The biggest problem is the furniture, which consists of two chests of drawers and a night table. I would like to do it myself, but I'm not sure what color. The bedspreads on the twin beds are a light brown.*

For a boys' bedroom with a southwest exposure, try a color scheme of orange, chocolate brown and white.

Paint your boys' furniture a bright orange and add white porcelain draw pulls to the chests of drawers. At the windows, hang chocolate brown and white big block checkered café curtains on brass poles. Walls can be a rich chocolate brown with eggshell white enamel trim and doors. The ceiling should be white. Use some checkered pillows on the brown spreads. A washable cotton rug in bright yellow would be my suggestion for the floor.

Question: *We have just finished decorating a large bedroom for our two college-age boys. It is paneled halfway in avocado, with upper walls and ceiling white. Carpet is a blue green tweed. What colors would you suggest for bedspreads and draperies? Would you use black or avocado furniture?*

The spreads on twin beds in a boys' room do not have to match.

Get your boys involved in the decorating. Maybe one boy would prefer an avocado spread and the other a royal blue spread. The draperies might be avocado and royal blue stripes on a beige linen background. For furniture I would prefer the black, but the boys might like the avocado. Either color furniture would look well.

Question: *My son picked out a zigzag pattern of green, blue, black and white for his bedspread. The walls of the room are white. My husband is building a desk and shelf unit in front of the window. What colors do you suggest for curtains, rug, and the unpainted study unit?*

Create a color scheme around the patterned fabric a boy chooses for his bedroom.

Your son sounds as though he has a real feeling for lively colors! The colors of his bedspread should be carried out in the rest of the room. Use the same pattern on window shades. Try to match the green in the bedspread in a rug peppered with black. Paint the exterior of the study unit the same shade of green, and for the interior shelves, I'd use a bright yellow. The desk chair can be painted blue to match the blue stripe in the bedspread.

The Bedroom

Question: *Can you tell me how to really brighten our bedroom? Right now the walls are pale blue, and the rug and curtains are white. The four-poster bed is painted white, with a white canopy and blue spread. There's a navy blue chair and a walnut desk, desk chair and night table. Everytime I walk into the room I feel as if I'm entering an iceberg. We are ready to change everything except the rug.*

Use soft pink, peach, melon and green to make a bedroom country-garden bright.

Yes, your bedroom could certainly stand some warmth. Pick the prettiest coordinate fabric you can find—perhaps one that features pink, peach and melon flowers with apple green leaves on a white background. Paper all your walls with this fresh bouquet, and use it for the spread, chair slipcover, curtains and valances. The bed canopy should be white muslin, as well as the dust ruffle.

Question: *I am planning to do my teenage daughter's room over. Everything goes except the furniture, which is white. I am planning on a lime green shag rug. What color should I use for the curtains and bedspread? There is an upholstered desk chair that could be recovered for a little added color.*

Lemon yellow, mauve pink, navy blue and lime green are exciting colors for a girl's room.

Paint your daughter's walls lemon yellow and the ceiling sky blue; trim should be white semigloss enamel. A perky lemon yellow, mauve pink, navy blue and lime green flowered print on a white ground would be delightful for her bedspread and draperies. Over the draperies, hang a shirred valance of the same fabric, and line it with lime green. Stain her floors a rich chocolate brown, and find that lime green shag rug. Her desk chair might be reupholstered in a bright shocking pink vinyl.

Question: *I plan to redecorate my sixteen-year-old daughter's bedroom, which is furnished in maple. She would like to paint the walls and woodwork blue. What shade of blue would you suggest? Also, what color should I use for the bedspread and throw rugs?*

Three different color schemes would work in a bedroom with blue walls: red, green and blue; shocking pink, green and blue; gold and blue.

I would suggest that you paint the bedroom walls a very pale sky blue and the woodwork and ceiling a sparkling clean white. On white rods with white rings, hang café curtains of a bright red and blue flowered print with green leaves on a white background. Carpet the room in brilliant red, and use the drapery print for the bedspread with a white dust ruffle. However, your daughter should express her likes and dislikes for both color and fabric design before you decorate the room. Perhaps she would prefer a shocking pink carpet with a shocking pink and green fabric at the windows and for bedspread. She might even prefer a gold carpet with a gold and blue damask fabric for her room's decor.

114

The Bedroom

Question: *The master bedroom in our Victorian house is enormous. For years I haven't given much thought to making it look more homey, but now I'd like to create a vanity-sitting area along the window wall. (This would be a good place for me to work uninterrupted on my crewel and needlepoint!) The walls of the bedroom are painted a peachy pink with white trim; the bedspread on the brass bed is white-on-white. Much of the hardwood floor is exposed but there is a beautiful Oriental area rug in shades of beige, red, blue and purple.*

Let the colors in an Oriental rug serve as the bridge to a whole new room area within a large bedroom.

Lucky you with your large Victorian bedroom and beautiful Oriental rug. The room, however, needs more life, and I'd take your color cues from the rug and splash them on your new vanity-sitting area. Look for a pink, purple, red and white crisscross pattern, and use it for your vanity skirt, lounge chair and tieback curtains. Beneath the curtains hang pink shades to match pink walls. Cover the vanity chair in luscious lavender or shocking pink velvet.

115

Question: *My husband built a trellis around the sleeping alcove in the guest room. We lacquered the trellis and all the wood furniture bright white. Now we are ready for color ideas. We'd like blue and a warm color.*

Use bittersweet for warmth with blue and white.

The two B's, bittersweet and blue, can be used together in an arbor of color for your guest room. Try a bittersweet, blue and white flowered print for your draperies and bedspread. Paint the woodwork white, but use the colorful print on your ceiling and walls. A bright bittersweet carpet will look lovely with the blue and white, as will bittersweet throw pillows.

The Bedroom

Question: *I just finished painting my young son's small bedroom a blueberry color. The floor is light green terrazzo. Bunk beds and a big chest of drawers are maple. I'd like to paint a desk, small chest and some bookshelves. Also, I want to make curtains and bedspreads. I like red, blue and white, but would like your color suggestions.*

An amusing green, white and blue print will brighten a boy's blue room.

With the light green terrazzo floor and blueberry walls, I would stay away from a lot of red, but hold onto your blue and white idea. Paint your desk, small chest and bookshelves a royal blue. Use new white porcelain knobs on the desk and chest of drawers. Select an amusing emerald green, royal blue, and white print for the bedspreads. I have seen a number of prints that delight little boys. One is called "Stop and Go" and is filled with colorful road signs. Hang café curtains of the print you select on blue poles with white wooden rings.

Question: *We have just moved into an apartment. The carpeting in the bedroom is grass green, and the walls are white. I have a beautiful bedspread with a dark turquoise design on a jade green background. Is there any way, working only with draperies, throw pillows, and slipper chair, that I could use my bedspread and still have a pretty room?*

Multicolor ribbons on each side of drapery panels can tie a bedroom's color scheme together.

I do not object to your turquoise and jade green spread with the grass green carpet. Why not hang white draperies at your windows with a three-color border along the side of each drapery panel? Sew grosgrain ribbons of jade green, mandarin orange and turquoise on the white draperies. Hang the white draperies under a white swag valance that is lined in mandarin orange; and use orange, turquoise and white pillows on your bedspread. You can substitute shocking pink or brilliant yellow for mandarin orange, if you prefer.

Question: *I'm at a loss about what to do with our bedroom. The bed-spread is blue and white toile. Our double dresser, night stand, and headboard are distressed country French. What color carpeting should we use? We would like a shag. Would you tell me what color we should use for draperies and walls?*

With a blue and white bedspread, why not use a blue and white stripe on the walls?

Why not paper your walls with a light blue and white stripe and paint all the woodwork eggshell white? At the windows, I would hang white draperies on a Wedgwood blue pole. Red—bright red—would be my suggestion for carpet. The pillows on your blue and white toile spread can be bright red and crisp white.

Question: *We are building a new house, and I need advice for decorating the master bedroom. The bedroom furniture is black with white rubbed very softly into the grain of the wood; the carpeting is gold. What would you suggest for color of walls, draperies and bedspread?*

Gold, black and white makes a dramatic bedroom scheme.

Why not paint your walls a clean white? Use a black and white printed linen damask at your windows under a white linen swag valance. The bed skirt can be the black and white damask and the spread white quilted linen. Sunny yellow, gold, white and melon throw pillows on the bed would be my recommendation for accessories, along with shiny brass night-table lamps with black opaque shades.

Question: *I have a bedroom with white carpeting and ceilings. I would like to do the walls, draperies and headboard in yellow and beige. Please tell me what color you would use for each. Also, please tell me what colors to add.*

A yellow, white and beige bedroom needs a touch of green to avoid the "vanilla" look.

Your bedroom sounds too bland. I would suggest you use a lettuce green, beige and yellow floral print on a white background for dra-

118

peries under a beige swag-and-jabot valance lined in bright yellow. Use the print for a bed skirt with a soft beige quilted spread. Pillow accents should be yellow and white. Use white lamps with shades made of the print to match your draperies. Paper your walls in a soft yellow and white stripe.

Question: *I would like a new color scheme for my bedroom. My furniture is antique white and gold French provincial and my rug is gold. I would like to keep my rug and furniture as they are. The walls are a corn silk yellow, but can be painted.*

Soft blue, white and gold spell serenity in a bedroom. Crystal accessories add elegance.

What about soft blue draperies with blue and white fringe under a pretty shaped valance, also fringed? Pretty embroidered-edge white sheer curtains would be nice. Walls can be painted a pale blue with white ceiling and woodwork. A quilted bedspread can be pale blue over a gold, white and blue striped bed skirt. The striped bed skirt fabric might also be used for throw pillows and for covering on a slipper chair. Crystal cut-glass lamps with white shades would be my choice for bedside lighting.

Question: *I am twelve years old and share a small room with an older sister. We would like the room done in royal blue and bright lime green. We have a white French provincial desk with two matching dressers, and white walls. Our bunk beds are maple. What color would you suggest for curtains, bedspreads and rug? Also, what color would you use for two chests I plan to antique?*

Add touches of pink to blue and green for a girl's bedroom.

Royal blue and lime green work wonderfully together, and even more so when a third color is added—such as pink. I suggest you find a pretty floral print in pink, royal blue and lime green for both curtains and bedspreads. A royal blue cotton shag rug on the floor would be my choice. For the perfect finishing touch, antique your two chests in lime green and outline the pieces in white.

Question: *My bedroom wallpaper is a gay print of red, yellow and blue on white. The bedspread and draperies are matching fabric. Should the canopy be the matching fabric, too? And what color should I look for in a new rug?*

Line a bed canopy with the rug color for a coordinated effect.

A canopy covered with your cheerful red, yellow and blue print will add interest and drama to your room. But for elegance and coordination, line the canopy with bright red, and then roll out a bright red carpet. If you have room for a bench at the foot of the bed, cover it in soft blue.

The Bedroom

Question: *We are building a home on a lake with many sliding-glass doors leading out onto the decks. One wall of the master bedroom will be sliding-glass doors opening onto a sunbathing deck. What colors should we use in the room so that it will look cozy, as a bedroom should, in spite of the steady light pouring in? Of course, we'll want draperies we can close over the door at night. Our bedroom furniture is Danish modern.*

Use the colors of summer in a bedroom that opens onto a sunbathing deck.

Pick a sunny summery color scheme that will be cheerful all year long, even when the decks are covered with winter's snow. I'd recommend a canary yellow cotton area rug and a modern geometric print for the bedspread. The geometric can be blue, yellow and cantaloupe on a white background. At your windows, hang white sheer draperies under a deck-design valance; the deck valance can be white canvas laced with yellow. I recommend openwork sheers so that you can see the view by day when the curtains are drawn. If you need blackout curtains, install them on a separate track behind the sheers.

Question: *I recently antiqued my bedroom set in pale blue. It is truly beautiful, but I am at a loss for colors for bedspread and throw rugs. I have purchased royal blue darkening shades and white ball-fringe curtains. My walls are white.*

Pale blue, royal blue and red make a delightful bedroom.

Your room sounds delightful to me—so far! What about a bright red bedspread? The skirt on your bed can be a bright pink, red, blue and white floral print. Buy enough of your bedskirt fabric to make some pillows for the bed. You can use a royal blue throw rug for your room, or a poppy red or shocking pink rug if you prefer.

Question: *I have new aqua carpeting and white draperies in my bedroom. How could I make it bright and cheerful? It needs more color.*

Fill out a white and aqua bedroom scheme with melon, emerald green and sky blue.

For your aqua and white bedroom, I'd suggest cheerful watermelon, emerald green, and sky blue floral draperies on a white background. I'd use a watermelon bed skirt on the bed with a quilted spread of the floral print. Throw pillows on the bed should be aqua and emerald green. I'd like to see you use white or aqua lamps with white shades.

Question: *We would like to redo our old blond bedroom set, perhaps antique it. What colors would you suggest for the bedroom set, draperies, walls and bedspread? Our bedroom carpet is blue, lavender and avocado.*

Paint an old bedroom set white lacquer, and trim it in emerald green.

Paint your bedroom set bright white lacquer, trimmed in brilliant emerald green. I would paint the walls a very soft sky blue with white trim. At your windows hang a fresh purple, green and white floral print on a white background. Use the same print for a quilted bedspread. A dust ruffle could be bright green for added bed interest.

Question: *My son wants bright yellows and greens in his room in our new house. It's not a very large room, but he wants it to be very grown-up and bold. Can you suggest a decorating scheme?*

Every boy likes boldly painted campaign furniture in his bedroom—the style adapted from the chests of early explorers.

Why not use black laminate campaign-style furniture in your son's room? Lay a black, emerald green and yellow tartan plaid rug. Tartan plaids make rooms look larger than they are. Cover the walls with sunflower yellow felt, and the window with matching yellow café curtains trimmed with green. Use a green corduroy for bolsters and bedspread; throw pillows can be yellow and black.

Question: *I love patchwork patterns, but I also love the blue, yellow and red stripe on my bedroom love seat. Can I use a patchwork print with these colors and still keep the striped love seat? My bed has a canopy. The floor is wide plank pine, mostly bare except for a blue shag oval rug.*

Patchwork patterns are gay, bold and comfortable; they look great with a stripe.

If you have a bent for patchwork, go all the way with it. Use the bright blue and yellow of your love seat as the patchwork colors, and put it on your walls, bed, windows, bedspread and canopy. Hang a back curtain of bright yellow behind the head of your bed. Accent the patchwork room with red borders on the curtains and bed. You might paint a bench or stool the same red and place it at the foot of your bed. I envy you such a colorful, comfortable room.

124

The Bedroom

Question: *Opening off our master bedroom through a single door is a lovely sitting room complete with marble fireplace. My husband and I both use this room a lot, leaving the downstairs to our three teenage children in the evenings. I'd like to redecorate the room mostly using white, but realize there should be a touch of another color. What do you suggest? Our bedroom is decorated in blue, beige and white.*

A decorating scheme of white and milk chocolate is the answer for a sitting room off the bedroom.

You're lucky to have such a hideaway room. Such an area is the ideal place to give in to your fondness for white, which in small doses is a restful, relaxing color. I would trim the draperies and upholstery with a simple border of chocolate brown. But do use a few accessories in bright yellow, blue and paprika orange.

125

The Bathroom

Hardly a day goes by that I do not see or hear about some new decorating idea for the bathroom. There are, of course, all those expensive things to do, like installing a marble sunken tub or gold-plated fixtures with dolphins and cherubs. We have all seen pictures of elegant bathrooms with hand-decorated washbowls, crystal chandeliers, flocked wall coverings, Austrian shades and elaborate drapery. And, of course, there are the French chairs, made of cane, to cover the toilet.

I am a great believer in bathroom decorating, but I do not say that one must go the marble and gold-plated fixture route. Decorating the bathroom can be fun and can be done successfully with color. The days of the antiseptic white bathrooms are gone, thank heavens! Not only are the basic fixtures available in a variety of colors, but homemakers today are going far beyond even these fixtures to bring color, warmth, and interest into the bathroom.

How do you create a color scheme for the bathroom? You start with the colors you cannot change in your present bathroom. That means that, unless you are building a new home or throwing out your tub, sink and commode, you start with the color of your present fixtures and probably the tile on the wall. With the new epoxy paints, however, you can change the color of your tiles. And if your sink is in bad shape, perhaps you could consider replacing it with a hand bowl in accent colors— lipstick red, sage green, buttercup yellow, royal blue. Hand bowls do not have to match the tub and toilet. In any case, you can build a color scheme that includes your fixtures and walls, ceiling, floor, window, shower curtain, towels and accessories.

Colors for your walls and ceiling are no longer limited to paint and a few dull "bathroom wallpapers." There is an almost endless variety of vinyl wall coverings that are washable, practical and easy to put up.

If you have a tile floor and like the colors, you can include them in your scheme or add a throw rug to introduce different colors. If your floor doesn't fit your scheme you can retile it in ceramic or vinyl tiles in lovely colors and patterns, you can paint it, or you can cover it in one of the dozen or so colors available in wall-to-wall bathroom carpeting.

Have you seen the exciting patterns and colors in indoor-outdoor carpeting now on the market?

Let your creative imagination run free when decorating your bathroom window. Shutters, venetian blinds, Austrian shades, curtains or roller shades; anything goes if it fits into your color scheme and decor. I am very keen on painted window shades. Painting shades is easy and fun to do. Paint only on shades that have a cloth back—never on all-plastic shades. Imagine how attractive your bathroom window would be with a do-it-yourself painted flower or design. Stenciling on shades is also easy to do with acrylic spray paint. Picture a shade with stars stenciled on it in a room with red, white and blue striped wall covering. Spray painting also makes striping easy on shades. Use ordinary masking tape on the shade to create the width of the stripe you want. When you remove the tape, you'll have a snappy striped shade.

Curtains can match your wall covering, your shower curtain or both. And speaking of shower curtains, remember that they are an important area of color in your bathroom. Any kind of cloth can be used, in any pattern or colors; simply hang a plastic curtain as a liner inside your cloth curtain.

There are so many towel colors and prints to choose from today that a visit to a store's linen department can inspire a bathroom color scheme. You can find towels that have coordinated rugs, shower curtains and window curtains to match. You can find prints that would be fun to reproduce on a window shade you paint yourself. If you feel timid about color in your bathroom, just look at the colors in today's bathroom linens, and cut loose from your old ideas.

Bathroom accessories are no longer limited to the soap dish and toothbrush cup. Today, bathroom accessories mean pictures on the wall, colorful and fanciful lighting fixtures, bright wastebaskets in unusual fabrics, flowers (yes, flowers!) and plants, hamper and chair or stool. Because the bathroom is usually a small room, the colors of the accessories play an important role in your scheme.

Just think of the fun you can have by indulging your sense of humor and whimsy. How about travel posters on the wall to look at while you lie dreaming in your tub? I recently saw a delightful bathroom decorated with bright travel posters. The carpet on the floor was a fire-engine red, as was the shower curtain. The shower curtain had large portholes at the top and at the bottom. One could take a shower and look out the upper portholes. One could also soak in the tub and look out at the pictures of faraway places. In this bathroom decor that was surely going places, the vanity cabinet was painted royal blue, as were lacquered louvered shutters at the window. Towels and bathmats were fire-engine red, royal blue and white.

You can create period styling with colors, fabrics and patterns. For example, wood tones on walls, floors and cabinets; Williamsburg blues and reds in wallpaper and accessories; colonial prints in the fabrics—all provide an Early American effect. Conversely, bold, dramatic colors, glass and chrome accessories, and bright geometric prints will help you create a modern-style bathroom.

You can go all-out with the wildest, way-out colors in a tiny powder room, or transform a "second thought" room into an exciting showplace that tells your guests you care.

Does the bathroom adjoin your bedroom? Coordinate the two rooms by repeating the bedroom's colors and patterns in the bathroom. Use the bedspread fabric for your shower curtain, and the bedroom wall colors for walls and towels of your bathroom.

Every room in your home reflects your personality, and the bathroom is no exception. Make it an integral part of the total picture of your decor. You have learned to use color in every other room. Now use color boldly in your bathroom.

Question: *Our bathroom fixtures and cabinets are white and are separated by wall partitions. The vanity counter top is green, the floor is green tile and the walls are white. This green and white combination strikes me as extremely cold and dull for a bathroom. Could you suggest another color for the walls?*

Rise and shine with a yellow, orange, green and white color scheme in the bathroom.

Your bathroom certainly needs perking up. It reminds me more of a hospital bathroom than a room in a home. First, you should cover the walls, including the partition, in a sun yellow washable vinyl. By all means consider covering your tile floor with marigold orange cotton carpeting. Towels can be green with orange, yellow or white monograms. If you have room and light, why not plant a handsome ironstone pot with lush green ferns?

130

The Bathroom

Question: *Our bathroom is a big problem because it is very dull and drab. The tile is medium light gray and covers the shower area completely, as well as the lower half of our walls and the floor. Our fixtures are all white. What colors would you use for upper walls, carpet and curtains?*

Yellow, pink and green are good colors to perk up a gray and white bathroom.

Go yellow, pink and green, and turn your drab bathroom into a bower of springtime. Cover your gray floor with a washable cotton shocking pink rug. Cover your walls above the tile with a sunny yellow, pink and green floral bouquet wallpaper. If you can find a coordinating fabric, use it as a shower curtain and, trimmed with a green and white braid, at your windows. Trim a white tissue box in the green and white braid; do the same to your wastebasket.

Question: *Our bathroom floor tile is gray with pale yellow, blue and pink dots; the lower half of our walls is white tile, as is our counter top. We have white fixtures and mahogany woodwork. What color should I paint the top half of the walls, and what color should I use for curtains, towels and wastebasket? Can pictures be hung on the walls?*

Pictures can lend color and interest to a bathroom as well as to other rooms.

First of all, paint your mahogany woodwork white semigloss enamel. Cover the walls above your tile with a sky blue and white striped self-adhesive vinyl, or with sky blue paint. Use a cheerful yellow shower curtain and matching yellow window curtain. Towels can be mixed: yellow bath towels, pink hand towels and blue face cloths. A pink wastebasket sitting on a yellow cotton bath rug would be most attractive. Finally, please do hang pictures on the walls. I firmly believe that pictures belong in every room of a home, except the closets!

Question: *The laminated plastic top of our bathroom vanity is pink with a gray and white design. Our floor is beige, speckled with a dark brown, gold, green and orange. Around the tub is a fairly dark green tile with a lighter green and white design through it. The tub and sink are white. What colors should we use for the shower and window curtains and for the walls? I love gold. Is there any way I could use this color?*

Gold works well with green tile and white fixtures.

Gold would not be a bad color with your beige, dark brown, gold, green and orange speckled floor. Nor would it look bad with your green tile and white fixtures. But your counter top has to go. It should be changed to a white plastic laminate. Then you can paint your walls a rich gold and your ceiling and woodwork clean bright white. Hang window curtains of a bright gold, melon and emerald green print on a white background. Use the print for your shower curtain over a plastic liner. Throw a gold washable cotton rug on your bathroom floor, and use emerald green bath towels, melon hand towels and white face cloths.

Question: *Our guest bathroom is off the hall, which is carpeted in gold. The floor and walls are tiled in white with black trim; the fixtures are white. I would like a suggestion for wallpaper. The area to be papered is very small. What colors should I use for the window curtain and bath accessories?*

Try mustard yellow, black and white for a sophisticated bathroom or powder room.

Mustard yellow, black and white is a sure-fire decorating scheme. How about checkered vinyl wallpaper in these colors for the small area to be covered? I take it that your window is small, also, so why not hang bright white painted louvered shutters. Towels can be bright mustard yellow and vibrant black. Accessories can be bright mustard.

The Bathroom

Question: *My bathroom is white. I mean,* all *white—fixtures, walls, floors. I want lots of color. The white tub and toilet must stay, but I could replace the wash bowl in its white vanity.*

African violet, blue and green will bring a bouquet of color into your bathroom.

Select a coordinate wall covering and fabric for walls, ceiling, window and shower curtains in shades of African violet, blue and green on a white background. Leave the base of your bathroom vanity white, but trim the moldings in African violet. A bright blue cotton shag rug on the floor would be one of the final notes of distinction; so would a blue hand bowl, if you decide to replace the white bowl.

Question: *My bathroom tile is very dark brown. The salmon pink floral wall covering above the tile is pretty enough to keep. The question: What color shower curtain, window curtain and rug should I use?*

A bathroom with dark brown tile requires color—perhaps orange, pink and white.

To begin with, I would suggest a bright orange carpet. Your shower curtain can be a pink and orange stripe on a white background. Shower curtain rings can be chocolate brown. At your windows, why not hang white curtains with an orange and chocolate brown ball fringe? Brass accessories in your bathroom would be my selection.

Question: *The bottom half of my bathroom wall is nutmeg-colored tile; the top half of the wall is painted the same color. The fixtures are tan. I have soft green carpeting on the floor. What color curtains should I use?*

A bright print of greens, chocolate and persimmon is the solution to a tan bathroom.

Sparkle up all that tan with a gay cotton curtain at the windows, maybe an emerald green, forest green, chocolate and persimmon garden print on a white background. Make a shower curtain of the same print, hung on white rings over a plastic liner. Towels can be pinky persimmon, chocolate, and emerald green.

Question: *I wish to brighten up my small bathroom with wallpaper. The fixtures are avocado, the carpet is gray green, and the window has a blue and silver reed blind. One wall is a mirror. What color and pattern can I use on other walls?*

The reflection in a mirrored bathroom wall should be interesting. Try a colorful print covering on the opposite wall and on the ceiling too.

On the walls and ceiling, I would use a bright flowered print featuring poppy orange, daffodil yellow, delphinium blue and avocado green on a white background. I would get a wall covering for which a matching fabric is available for your shower curtain. Towels can be melon with delphinium blue; and for a change-off, daffodil yellow with avocado.

Question: *I need help with a problem bathroom that has peach tiles on lower walls with a butterscotch feature strip. Fixtures are white. The vanity top is white with metallic gold specks; the floor tile is white speckled with black. What color shall I paint upper walls and ceiling? What colors would be appropriate for carpeting, accessories and towels?*

Here's a color scheme for a peach bathroom: apricot, aqua blue and emerald green.

Paint your walls a pale aqua blue. The ceiling and trim can be bright white. Towels should be apricot and aqua blue. For accessories— tissue holder, cup and wastepaper basket—go bright emerald green. On the floor, choose an aqua blue cotton shag carpeting.

Question: *What color window curtain, bath rug and upper wall would go with a pink tiled bathroom? The wall tile has a burgundy trim. The walls above the tile presently are painted aqua. The fixtures are white, and the floor is tiled in yellow and pink blocks.*

Tile trim the wrong color? Paint it out with epoxy or marble paint.

A combination of pink, burgundy, aqua, yellow and white doesn't spell too much color harmony. Get rid of the burgundy trim by painting it a clean white with epoxy paint. Cover your aqua walls with a pretty pink, lemon yellow, and green flowered washable vinyl. The shower curtain and window curtain can be sunny yellow to coordinate with yellow hand towels. Bath towels and face cloths can be pastel pink or white.

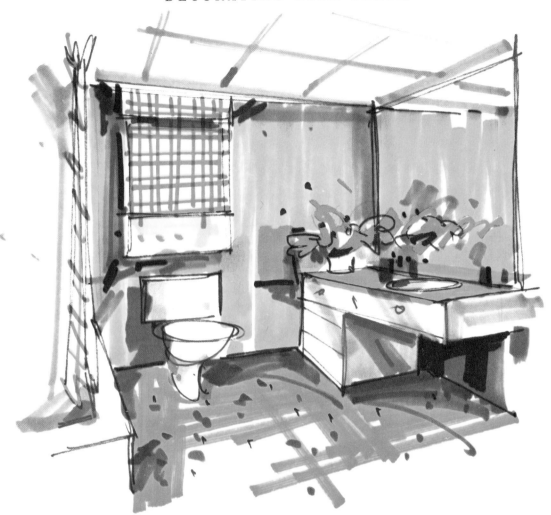

Question: *The bathroom in our new cooperative apartment is about as sterile looking as you can imagine. The fixtures are white, the floor is beige tile and the walls are covered with a beige grass cloth vinyl which is washable. Actually, the wall covering is quite handsome—even though it is beige—and we would like to keep it. How can we otherwise add some color to this room?*

Pumpkin and avocado, added to beige and white, livens a drab bathroom.

Assuming your bathroom has a window, I'd hang a Roman shade in a crisscross plaid design that features avocado and pumpkin on a white background. Use the same fabric and design for a shower curtain. For that special decorator touch, why not install a pumpkin-colored laminated plastic counter top on your bathroom vanity?

136

The Bathroom

Question: *So far my bathroom is white and black: white fixtures, white walls, white floor tiles trimmed with black and a white vanity with a counter top of black and white marbleized plastic laminate. What should I use for a third color, and where should I use it? I am generally opposed to bathroom carpeting.*

The black, white and pink bathroom is a favorite of many.

Why not hang a pink moiré vinyl on your walls? Paint the vanity cabinet pink semigloss enamel, and trim the cabinet molding in black or apply black molding. The shower curtain, over a plastic liner, should also be pink moiré. For towels and bathmats, I'd recommend pink, white and black.

Question: *We would like to remodel our first floor bathroom. A new sink will be built into a cabinet. Our problem is that the bathtub and stool (on the same side of the room) are lavender! What colors could we use in decorating this room? The rest of our home is done in white, brown and beige with green accents.*

A bathroom's colors can be painted on the inside of a round white sink for a dramatic touch.

For a great wall covering, choose a mauve pink, lime green and pale lavender print on silver foil. This rich color scheme is an exciting background for your lavender fixtures. Select a round sink and paint it (first with a primer coat, then with epoxy) a lavender shade to match other fixtures. The counter top and splash back can be a marbleized formica that has lots of gray lines running through it. Cabinets can be a gray white color. Towels might be deep lavender and bright lime green.

Question: *My very small bathroom has light mint green tile halfway up the walls. The fixtures are white. I would like a cozy and cheerful look, since my taste is Early American. What colors would you suggest for upper walls, floor, curtains, shower curtain, towels and toilet seat cover?*

A bathroom can take a checkered patterned wall covering.

Find a vinyl wall covering with a 2-inch check in mint green and bright white. Don't use a curtain at your small window. Instead, hang bright white painted louvered shutters with shiny brass pulls. The shower curtain can be bright white cotton with a plastic liner behind it. Sew onto your shower curtain a 2-inch wide mint green ribbon and a 2-inch wide apricot ribbon down the front edge and along the bottom edge. Be sure to leave at least a 1-inch space between the ribbons. Towels can be mint green and apricot. Floor covering might be a white brick vinyl tile. Use an apricot shag throw rug on the floor, and the toilet seat cover can be apricot also.

The Bathroom

Question: *The bathroom between my daughter's and son's bedrooms is most uninteresting. Everything is white except the black and white parquet-type floor. I can change the walls and vanity, but I'm unable to figure out what color would go well with the adjoining bedrooms. My daughter's bedroom is yellow and blue; my son's is chocolate, tan and white with touches of red.*

Consider a restful blue in a bathroom that connects two bedrooms.

A lovely sky blue added to your black and white bathroom should solve the problem. Cover both walls and ceiling with a blue on white floral or damask pattern. Of course, the covering should be washable. Paint the lower portion of the bathroom vanity pale blue, and trim it with black molding. If you want the blue, white and black bathroom to be accented with another color, I'd suggest a green plant or two.

Question: *Are pink and lavender suitable for a bathroom? Those are the colors in my bedroom, and I'd like to coordinate the color schemes of the two rooms. The bathroom fixtures are white.*

A bedroom's colors can be carried over into an adjoining bathroom— if they are your favorite colors.

Pink and lavender are the favorites of many women and can certainly be the color scheme for the bathroom. Consider pale pink vinyl-covered walls with lavender trim. Use a lavender cotton shag rug on the floor. The shower curtain can be pale pink, trimmed with luscious lavender braid or fringe.

140

The Bathroom

Question: *The lower half of the walls in our bathroom is tiled in gray and the floor is gray and coral tiles. The fixtures are a light peach tone. There is a vanity counter in black and white marbleized formica, with two wooden drawers underneath the counter in natural birchwood. The tub is glass enclosed. What should we do with the upper walls and ceiling? Should we paint the wooden drawers? What color towels and what window treatment would you advise?*

Black and white flowered wall covering sets the style in a coral and gray tiled bathroom.

Use a black and white flowered wall covering on the ceiling and on the walls above the gray tile. Paint the wood below your counter top a bright white lacquer. Lay an apple green cotton shag rug on your floor. At your window, I would use louvered shutters lacquered white. Towels can be black, lettuce green and vibrant melon. Bathroom accessories can be lettuce green.

Question: *I don't know what to do with our bathroom. The lower walls are light yellow ceramic tile. The fixtures are light beige, and the floor is a dark brown ceramic tile. Do you have any suggestions for curtains and upper half of the walls?*

Create a tent effect on the ceiling of your bathroom with wall covering in stripes of the room's colors.

Your beige, yellow and brown colors are all in the same family. Why not consider a striped vinyl wallpaper of these colors above the tile? If your ceiling fixture is in the center of the room, continue the stripe across the ceiling from all four sides, tapering off at the fixture. Be sure to miter the corners. Your end result will be a tent effect—lots of fun for a bathroom. Paint all the trim a chocolate brown, low luster enamel. For the window treatment, make a shade by gluing the wallpaper over a regular roller shade. Towels can be a bright orange and a rich chocolate brown.

Question: *My bathroom fixtures are blue, floor tiles are blue and white, the ceiling is white, the walls are pink and the curtains are blue. I want to change the color of the walls; what do you suggest?*

Mattress ticking stripes are great on bathroom walls.

The new vinyl wall coverings include mattress ticking stripes in many colors. For a striking bathroom, I'd suggest a yellow and white ticking stripe. If you care to redecorate further, what about a sky blue floral print on a white background for curtains at your window? Use the same print for shower curtains with canary yellow rings.

Question: *How can I perk up our pink and blue bathroom? The fixtures are pink and the tile is blue, with blue and white paper above the tile. What color carpeting and towels would you suggest?*

Try kelly green carpet to perk up a pink and blue bathroom.

Put a little excitement in your life. Try bright kelly green carpeting on your floor, with kelly green and shocking pink towels. On your shower rod, hang a curtain of kelly green, shocking pink and sky blue flowered print on a white background. Shower rod rings can be snappy shocking pink. Buy some shocking pink wicker pieces—perhaps a wastebasket, a tissue holder and a coaster glass holder.

Question: *The lower half of our bathroom is tiled in aqua; upper walls are painted a lighter aqua. The fixtures and floor are white. There is one window. What do you suggest for more color?*

Use plaid curtains to add life to a bathroom.

I suggest that you paint your upper walls a bright, clean white and your ceiling shocking pink. All the trim can be the same aqua color as your tile. Towels should be white and shocking pink. At your window, hang a shocking pink, white, and aqua plaid fabric. Perhaps you could shirr the fabric top and bottom in the opening of an aqua painted wooden shutter frame.

The Bathroom

Question: *I want to completely redecorate our bathroom, which is presently mostly white with pale yellow walls and vanity. Of course we'll keep the tub and toilet white, but I want to put color everywhere else. Can you suggest a color scheme that uses strong bright colors, with white as an accent only?*

Use three strong colors in bathroom decorating for an up-to-date look.

Bright red, bright green, and bright blue can be used most effectively together, especially in a bathroom where you might least expect it! Find an elegant wallpaper that features red, green, blue and touches of black with a little bit of white background showing through. Cover your vanity counter top in bright blue laminated plastic with a lipstick red accent bowl. Paint the cabinet base with black semigloss enamel. Black gives weight and special distinction to this bathroom setting. Cotton shag carpeting on the floor could be bright red, bright green or bright blue. A wise homemaker could and would alternate the colors of a shag rug.

Question: *My bathroom has yellow walls, a white linoleum floor and white fixtures. It is a perfectly acceptable room, but I'd like to get some color into it—perhaps in the towels and even the floor. What colors would you suggest?*

Get a variety of reds into a yellow and white bathroom.

Style your bathroom with modern colors—bright red, orchid, shocking pink—to go with your yellow walls. I'd lay bright red linoleum on the floor, and then cover that—leaving a substantial border—with an orchid cotton rug. Your towels can be plum and pink, and if you have a vanity stool, why not paint it pink semigloss enamel?

144

The Family Room and Den

The family room is truly "all things to all men." Every member of the family finds different uses for it. It's a hobby room, a game room, a sewing room, a TV room. Same thing with a den, which is actually a small family room. A den is a library, a study room, a guest bedroom, even a business office.

All this versatility presents certain challenges and problems in decorating. Today's modern, active family requires a room that can take a lot of use and abuse; therefore, family room and den furnishings and upholsteries must be tough and practical. The choice of furnishings will result from the activities for which the room is to be used. But the mood, the style, the "feel" of your room reflects your family's life style. Your success in expressing this life style is determined by your ability to use color well.

Let's look at some of the problems you must keep in mind when selecting a color scheme for a family room or den. All the considerations that apply to other rooms must be accounted for here. Too-small rooms must be opened up with proper use of color. Too-high ceilings should be brought down with color. These kinds of problems have been dealt with in other chapters. But the family room and den are unique, and some of its decorating challenges are also unique.

Your family room may be connected with your kitchen or dining room, and you may wish to coordinate the colors of the two rooms. It may be in the basement, and this will call for light, bright colors. Perhaps it is a porch or sunroom that is open to much light and air; this, too, has to be considered in planning a color scheme.

Is it a completely new room you are decorating? Then your choice of colors depends on your taste. Or do you have a family room or den that is the catchall for the furniture rejects from other rooms or from relatives? Then your use of color is even more challenging, for in this case your colors have to unify and coordinate, renew and restore a possibly unrelated assortment of furniture, fabrics, carpets.

I think the greatest difficulty in choosing family room or den decor stems from the nicest thing about these rooms—they are used by all the family, and they are used for casual, informal living. You may take into account each person's color preferences; you can even consult each one about his color ideas. But, let's face it, since only one color scheme can be used, *you* are going to have to decide what colors are best for the room. If the room ends up with a warm, welcoming color scheme, everyone is going to be happy with it.

I'd like to emphasize that last point. This room, by its very nature, must be warm, friendly and relaxed if it is to succeed. If the kids can't flop down on sturdy furniture or on the floor and play games, if Dad can't kick off his shoes and have a snack while watching TV, if Mom can't cut out a pattern and not worry about snips of material falling to the floor— then the family will never feel this room to be its own. The feeling of ease cannot be achieved, for instance, in a room with a pale, subdued, monochromatic color scheme. Nor will it be found in a room whose colors and textures create a formal, dignified atmosphere.

One of the nicest ways to provide warmth is with wood paneling, and I suppose that is why so many family rooms and dens are paneled. You can use wormwood-like plywood or a light walnut or any of the many beautiful wood grains on the market: elm, birch, mahogany, fruitwood. Remember, however, that the wood of the walls becomes a major color in the room's total scheme.

Not every family room or den need be mellow and woody. There are many looks to choose from—Mediterranean styling, French, English, colonial American—whatever style and mood you find most relaxing. One of my favorite family room styles is what I like to call the conservatory. The conservatory is a light and bright room for all kinds of fun. It often resembles a greenhouse, because it is styled in nature's fresh colors and textures. I use lots of white and fresh apple green, then add excitement with touches of orange. White wicker furniture and plenty of healthy green plants in clay pots help build the outdoors feeling. I may even add a small tree or two set in natural straw baskets.

As you know by now, through the pages of this book, I feel that accessories and appointments are keys to good decorating. Not only does this apply especially to the family room or den, but the whole concept opens up new vistas for personalized decor in this special room. Here your accessories can directly reflect the interests and personalities of your family. If sailing is your bent, hang a sailboat over your family room sofa, with some attractive nautical prints and nautical accessories. If riding is your preferred sport, a collection of china, metal, wood or papier-mâché horses on wood brackets can be the thing. If horticulture is your interest, hang an array of pressed flowers in colorful frames on that wall over the sofa or over the television set.

Rows of books on handsome shelves lend a room lots of color, but books in the family room or den can do more than provide warm, interesting color. Here you can house those books that relate to family interests. Mom's gardening and cookbooks may occupy a place on the shelves, along with Dad's books on hunting, fishing, automobiles or whatever.

One of my friends turned an old armoire into a bookcase for his family room, and it was most interesting and exciting. The armoire was painted a royal blue with white trim, and the shelves and background fire engine red. The red, white and blue armoire certainly worked with his family room decor.

Whatever you call the room—be it family room, den, rumpus room, "rec" room, TV room—it must have a color scheme that will ensure its use as your family's activity center.

Question: *I am antiquing a desk in Wedgwood blue and plan to decorate a den around this desk. The room has two small windows. Color suggestions for walls, rug, draperies and other furnishings will be greatly appreciated.*

Brown felt walls and white woodwork provide a new, exciting background for a den.

How about chocolate brown felt on your walls with white semigloss enamel for the trim and flat white for the ceiling? Felt now comes with a paper backing which makes it easy to hang. The floor might be a rich chocolate brown and white geometric or plaid carpet. For your sofa and draperies, choose a sky blue, white and chocolate brown patterned fabric. Throw pillows for the sofa can be lemon yellow, sky blue and emerald green. A white lacquered Parsons table next to your sofa and a square steel and glass coffee table in front of the sofa would be nice. Club chairs might be upholstered in white leather or vinyl.

Question: *Our family room has two walls paneled in pecan; one wall is white brick with a door in the center and a small window on each side of it. All the furniture is upholstered in black naugahyde. Please help me with rugs and draperies, as we are obviously living with a blah room.*

Black naugahyde furniture in a family room or den needs colorful rugs and curtains.

Your family room does need help, and color is the answer. Use a rug with a geometric design in a combination of bright reds, cerulean blues and lime greens. The rug might have a rich red border. Hang white curtains at your windows under a red damask print on a white linen valance. Line your curtains in lime green. Use red, cerulean blue and lime green pillows on your sofa. Hang many colorful modern prints on your walls. Red end table lamps would be my choice, or brass lamps with white shades.

The Family Room and Den

Question: *Our family room is paneled in driftwood gray, the fireplace wall is natural brick and the floor slate gray flagstone. I plan to buy a rug and recover two wing chairs and four dining chairs for this room, but I need advice on color.*

Use a rug of many soft colors to soften the look of a family room's stone floor.

You need to add warmth to all that wood, brick and stone, and color is the answer. On your flagstone floor lay a large area rug with a champagne beige background and lots of soft blue, green and tomato red in the pattern. Upholstering the wing chairs in a rich buttercup yellow naugahyde would bring a lot of glow into your family room, too. Dining chairs can be covered in the same yellow naugahyde. Hang lots of bright paintings or prints on your walls.

Question: *The furniture in my den-office includes a glass-top desk, white naugahyde club chair, black naugahyde swivel chair and a white throw rug. I need another chair, but can't decide on the color. Also, what color can I paint the walls and woodwork? I want to achieve an atmosphere of comfort in spite of the modern furnishings.*

For a den-office in which anyone would feel at home, paint the walls a rich grass green.

A den in which you'll be doing some work should definitely be easy on the eyes. I suggest you paint your walls Kentucky bluegrass green, and woodwork white semigloss enamel. For an unexpected touch of the traditional in the midst of your modern furnishings, buy a wing chair in mandarin orange; the orange will add a lot of dash to the setting. Behind the desk, hang a print of an ancient map in a thin brass frame.

Question: *Some furniture from our old home will go into furnishing a hobby room in our new house: A chest of drawers, a china closet and some dining room chairs. This room will be used for sewing, painting and flower arranging. What finish and color would you suggest for the old furniture and what would be a good wall color? My favorite color is yellow.*

Try yellow and white lacquer for decorating magic on old furniture.

If your favorite color is yellow, lacquer your old furniture in daffodil yellow. I would trim the pieces in bright white lacquer. Paint the back portion of your china cabinet and drawer interiors a rich melon or a lettuce green. Get some new shiny brass hardware for your drawer pulls. Cover the seats of your dining room chairs in a lettuce green, melon, yellow and sky blue print on a white background; use the print for window draperies too. Paint your walls melon and the trim and ceiling white.

Question: *Our small den has a northern exposure and a beautiful view of a river through double sliding-glass doors. The walls are antique white and the carpeting is beige. Please advise me as to other colors for the room. I'd like to achieve an Oriental look.*

White, black and red is the color scheme for an Oriental look.

On your sliding-glass doors, hang white and black bamboo roller blinds. The blinds will help level the light but will not close out your view of the river. Hang a beautiful black, white and red three-panel Oriental screen on one of your walls over a red lacquered Chinese commode. The commode should have large brass Oriental hardware. Use a rich lime-colored sofa or love seat in the room with black teak end tables. White Oriental Foo-dog lamps would be my choice, with white nubby fabric shades. The coffee table can be Oriental in feeling, and it would look handsome on a red, black and beige Oriental rug. A large jade plant in an Oriental porcelain tub would further enhance your Far East setting.

Question: *The family room in the new home we are building will have white imitation brick walls. One wall has two regular sized windows with white shutters; the opposite wall has built-in cabinets and shelves. We have a mustard gold shag rug for the floor. We need help in choosing colors for a couch, two matching chairs and maybe a pull-up chair.*

Add black to mustard gold and white for a spicy family room.

A black vinyl-covered couch against one white brick wall would look stunning. Cover matching armless chairs trimmed with chrome or stainless steel in black and mustard gold stripe. An inexpensive black canvas-covered director's chair is your best bet for a pull-up chair. Two clear plexiglass cubes on the shag rug would make ideal tables in front of the couch or beside the matching chairs. Gold and white are the colors for throw pillows on your couch. Brass lamps with white shades would be my choice for lights.

Question: *How can I make our family room dramatic? It is long, dark and has fruitwood paneled walls. What color sofa, chairs and rug should I use to brighten it up? My draperies are off-white casement cloth. I also have five children who watch TV and play in the room often.*

Make a monotonous family room come alive with a colorful plaid or an argyle pattern.

Plaids seem to be in this year—and every year. So why not select a very practical one with a lot of pizazz? I would recommend a bright Confederate blue, apple red and sunny yellow plaid or argyle pattern for your sofa. Use a bright red nylon or vinyl fabric on your chairs. Dash up the sofa with bright red and yellow toss cushions. Add that drama to your windows with a red valance, lined in plaid argyle, over your off-white draperies. A royal blue cotton shag area rug would be my practical choice for the floor to cut down the sound of ten pattering feet.

The Family Room and Den

Question: *I want our den to be quiet, serene and sedate, but I also want it to have brightness and cheer. Can I have both in a color scheme? One wall consists of bookshelves with lots of books, plus two windows. The floor is beige vinyl tile.*

A champagne beige, white and tomato red color scheme is both soothing and bright for a den.

The fact that you have lots of books means you're well on your way toward achieving the quiet yet cheerful look for your den. I would consider for your floor a Mexican area rug in a combination of black, white, brown and beige. Paint your walls beige and your bookshelves beige with white interiors. Cover the sofa in a soft, glovelike white vinyl. Library chairs in the den should be covered in tomato red nylon for the brightness you want. Use the red for sofa pillows, for the mat around a hunting print that is framed in black and gold, for an ashtray or two.

Question: *We are adding a family room to our house which will be all windows on three sides. I shall use venetian blinds; should they be in a color? Tell me colors for the one wall, the furniture and perhaps an area rug.*

For the sunniest family room in town, use the brightest shades of yellow and orange with lots of white.

Your walls should be a clean white. Since your venetian blinds are a good portion of your walls, they should be white, too. Use a print of orange, yellow and green on a white background at your windows. Upholster your furniture in bright orange nylon, accent the sofa with pillows to match the curtains, if you wish. On the floor I'd suggest an area rug of bright yellow with bright orange blocks.

154

Question: *I have a small sewing-sitting room where I make most of the family's clothes. I am in the process of redecorating the room to make it lighter, as the work I do here is hard on my eyes and I need all the light I can get! I have so far used nothing but white; I've laid a white vinyl floor, painted the walls white, and painted an old wicker chaise lounge and wicker table a glossy white. Now: where do I add color? I want just one color with the white.*

Ultramarine blue and white is a striking color combination and is especially appropriate for a room where eyestraining work is done.

Bring color to your room by painting the doors and window ultramarine blue with semigloss enamel. You might paint the baseboards the same blue, too, and your sewing table and chair. Then, upholster your wicker furniture in an ultramarine blue and white floral print. Use the same print fabric for your curtains and perhaps a table skirt.

Question: *The family room in our basement is so uninviting that no one in the family uses it very much. Hopefully, I can change this by doing some inexpensive redecorating. The concrete floor is presently painted black and the plaster walls are painted white. There's an old round table and four chairs, a sofa covered in a gray tweed and a red corduroy armchair. The sofa could be slipcovered, but the chair material is in good shape.*

Paint a basement family room floor a vibrant color and you're off to a good start.

To begin with, why not paint that concrete floor a rich blue? Install a dado around the walls and paint it the same blue. Cover the walls above the dado with a yellow and white striped vinyl. The stripes on two walls should be vertical; on the other two walls, the stripes should be horizontal. Paint your table white and your chairs yellow. Slipcover the sofa in a gay floral red, yellow, blue and green on a white background. Area rugs can be pale yellow and white stripes, or fake beige fur.

Question: *We have a picture window the width of our family room. Under the window is a built-in couch. I thought the couch cushions would look great in red. Would felt wear well on the cushions? They get a lot of wear. What color would be best for curtains, and a new rug?*

Bright red vinyl is warm and practical for family room furnishings.

For a family room that gets a lot of use, I would use bright red vinyl on the cushions. Vinyl will stand up very well. Perhaps you can use red felt for café-type curtains in the room and a cherry red and billiard green hound's-tooth carpeting or area rug. Throw some yellow and green pillows on the sofa.

Question: *We are going to turn a large part of our basement into a family room for us and our three teenage children. We are starting with rough white plaster walls and ceiling, four windows which provide very little light, a concrete floor and some worthless furniture from a farm auction—namely, a comfortable sofa and armchair and a rocking chair. What colors should I use everywhere, including new slipcovers for furniture?*

Consult teenage children about color preferences for a new family room.

It is always important to consult children when decorating a room they will be using. You want your teenagers to feel the family room is very much *theirs*. I'm sure they will go for "now" colors, and you should, too. But in case your family is "color stumped," I suggest sunshine yellow walls, a white ceiling, and a barn red floor. Leave part of the floor bare for dancing; cover the rest with a salt and pepper carpet. Slipcover the sofa in a floral pattern of yellow, poppy red and green on a white background, the chair in a solid green corduroy. See if the rocker isn't worth stripping and staining a rich walnut brown. For an unusual coffee table get three tires from your local garage which are no longer usable. Paint one yellow, one red and one white. Stack them on top of each other, and place a piece of plate glass over the tires. Presto, the perfect coffee table for a well-used family room!

The Family Room and Den

Question: *I want to use brown and copper colors in our family room. How can I use these colors without getting a dreary room? What colors should I use for accents? I'm going to slipcover my couch and club chairs and paint the walls.*

Brown shades are fine for family room or den as long as you accent with bright warm colors.

Why not select a beige, chocolate brown and white plaid for your couch and club chair? Cover the other chair in chocolate brown. Paint your walls a copper brown, beige or mocha brown. Be sure to use lots of accent color to add zest to your room. Some good ones would be mandarin orange, emerald green and canary yellow.

Question: *Our den needs color. It is paneled in knotty pine. There are three separate windows with pull-down shades in sand and white striped oilcloth; a yellow and gold vinyl couch and two black deck chairs with canvas covers that need replacing. I want new indoor-outdoor carpeting and one new chair.*

For a daring den, cover deck chairs with leopard spots.

Re-cover your black deck chairs in a leopard patterned heavyweight vinyl. I've seen several good-looking ones on the market. For your new chair, how about a mandarin orange, grass green and white stripe? Perhaps a sailcloth fabric would be nice. On your yellow gold couch, place some fun vinyl-covered throw pillows. I suggest you look for a shocking pink and mandarin orange geometric for one, and perhaps a lime green patent for another. Carpet your family room with grass green indoor-outdoor carpet.

Question: *We have just bought a Colonial-style house with a small room off the kitchen which we intend to use as a family room. The walls are paneled in pine, though one wall is taken up by a brick fireplace and recessed bookshelves. The problem with the room is lack of light. There is only one window; it faces north, and right outside there is a blue spruce we don't want cut down. How do you suggest we make the room bright and cheerful? The only furnishings we have for the room so far are a braided rug in shades of orange, yellow and rust, a brown vinyl recliner chair, and my husband's collection of prints of sailing ships. We don't want to spend much money on the family room, as we have already put a lot of money into furnishing the rest of the house.*

Pine-paneled family rooms call for the lightest, brightest colors.

I like pine paneling, but it can make a room very dark, especially when there are few or no windows. You are going to have to achieve lightness and brightness with color, and with lamps. Find a comfortable secondhand sofa and cover it with solid bright yellow; put throw pillows on the sofa in solid orange and blue and one in a yellow, orange, green and blue plaid on a white background. Put the same plaid pillow on the brown recliner chair. Instead of traditional end tables or coffee table, go in for white lucite cubes on either side of the sofa or a glass-top coffee table. An occasional chair can be something picked up at a thrift shop or auction and painted bright orange. If you need to put anything over your window—and it doesn't sound as though you have to—consider an orange and beige striped shade. Lamps in the room should have very white shades. Your husband's prints grouped together on one wall will add a light touch.

Question: *The upholstered pieces in our family room are covered in an apple green, shocking pink and red crisscross plaid fabric. These are the colors I want in the rest of the room, but I don't know where to put which. Can you suggest which colors for walls, draperies, ottoman and area rug?*

Fresh apple green, shocking pink and red is a great color scheme. Add purple and white to make it even greater.

Paint your walls apple green and your ceiling white. Woodwork, such as doors, crown moldings and baseboard can be stained walnut for the feeling of hominess and solidity you want in a family room. I would suggest a red floral pattern on a green background for your window draperies. For the area rug find a shocking pink, purple and white stripe or geometric print in washable cotton. Your ottoman and throw pillows can be a pink and purple print on white.

The Foyer and Hall

The foyer entrance welcomes you, your family, your visitors. It is the first area one sees upon opening the door. It sets the tone for the house and describes the kind of people who live in it. I have always advocated bold use of color in decorating, and I feel that the foyer is a good place to start. Your foyer can be bright and cheerful with sunshine colors; it can be sophisticated and exciting with a dramatic color scheme. Color can help you create a period style foyer—for example, for the colonial minded a clay-colored herringbone brick pattern on the floor, and on the walls, a paper featuring Revolutionary soldiers in golds, reds and royal blue on a Wedgwood blue background. And think of how exciting today's Now color schemes—apple green and deep royal blue, or plum, shocking pink and lemon yellow—would look in a foyer.

Today's homes usually have small foyers, and for them I generally recommend sunny, soft colors and open design wall coverings. Mirrors are another way to expand space visually. Sheet mirror has found a real home in foyer decorating. Many times I have mirrored all the walls and doors in a small foyer. On the floor I often use alternating stripes of white and black tiles. The stripes are reflected in the mirrors, thus creating the illusion that the foyer is bigger than it actually is.

A welcoming foyer contains some basic pieces: a table, shelf or chest to hold mail, flowers, pocketbooks, gloves and whatever; bench or chair to sit on when putting on winter boots or when waiting for the car to come; a mirror for touching up makeup and setting a hat straight. The colors of these pieces can determine whether your foyer looks crowded and small, or large and airy. Do they blend into the background colors and seem to recede? Or are they in sharp contrast to the foyer's colors and stop the eye so that they seem larger?

When foyer decorating, consider your needs and be practical. If you have several children who tramp in and out of the door several times a day, all year long, then for goodness sake, do not use a light carpet in the foyer. Pick some practical color or select an easily cleaned vinyl in a color that will work into your foyer color scheme. There are so many kinds of flooring treatments that can be considered when planning the foyer for a new or redecorated home. Think about carpeting, wood boards, terra cotta, quarry tiles, the endless varieties of marbles and slates in a great assortment of colors.

I love foyers that feature fresh flowers for a lovely touch of color. In the fall, a pot of chrysanthemums would be my suggestion. In the winter or at Christmas, poinsettias, star-of-Bethlehem plants or pots of holly would be timely. Springtime tulips and jonquils, or a vase of lilacs or forsythia would be a joyful greeting for that lovely season. When summer rolls around, an arrangement of cut garden flowers, doubling in the mirror behind it, is sure to spell welcome in the foyer of any home.

Don't treat your foyer as the stepchild of your home. Give it the same care when decorating as you do any other room. And, as in any other room, be certain to coordinate with color all your foyer materials—wall treatment, floor treatment, fixtures and furniture. Each element should fit into the color scheme you plan for this room.

If the foyer is the introduction to your home, the hallway is the connecting link. Have you ever walked through a home and seen beautiful rooms all connected by an uninteresting corridor? I have, and many times.

Recently, I planned the design and decoration of a new home in the country just outside Englewood, New Jersey. The house featured a major color—bright red—with accent colors of cocoa brown, white, sunshine yellow and lime green. The home was all on one level. The living room, dining room and kitchen were all to the right; the bedrooms, nursery and baths, all to the left off a long hallway. For the hallway decor, cocoa brown and red grass cloth was used on the walls, and all the doors facing the hall were painted fire engine red semigloss enamel with white semigloss enamel door frames. With a red carpet and white Plexiglas hanging fixtures, the hallway came alive and coordinated with the rest of the house.

There are lots of ways to make a long narrow hallway seem wider and shorter, such as the horizontal stripe method. Vinyl tiles should be laid in alternating stripes from wall to wall. You might add sunshine to a dark windowless hallway with bright canary yellow and white 12-inch vinyl tiles on the floor. Paint your walls a sunshine yellow, or cover them with sunshine yellow felt above a white dado. Fill the walls with many colorful prints and accessories.

If you are a good coordinator, you might paint the hallway doors in your home different bright colors. For example, why not paint Junior's

162

door a royal blue? Sis's door can be shocking pink, and the doorway to the master bedroom a rich sunshine yellow. Tie the whole scheme together with plaid wall covering of royal blue, shocking pink and yellow on a white background. Lay a bright yellow carpet on the floor.

Hallways with windows offer the homemaker a chance to do something exciting with window decor. Why not consider a greenhouse at your hallway window? Install glass shelves on brackets across the entire width of the window, and fill the shelves with exciting plants—ivy, ferns and bulb varieties that will blossom all year long. I like hallway windows that have window seats. Then you will have a place to sit and enjoy the lovely colors of your hallway and, perhaps, your garden view.

Remember that your hallway should not be simply a way of getting from one room to another. There should be points of interest, color, and beauty enroute. In fact, the hall is a great place to hang pictures or a collection of framed photographs from the family album. And if the hallway is wide enough, consider bookshelves on one side for your overflow of books.

Question: *We would like to repaper our foyer, which is presently papered with a gold mottled design. The floor is inlaid linoleum in shades of gold. As you enter the foyer, to the right is a large, rectangular oil painting of an autumn landscape. To the left is a table with an oval mirror in a gold frame above it. The whole effect now is stuffy and dull. What wallpaper do you suggest?*

Let the colors in a favorite painting be your foyer decorating guide.

Why not be inspired by the colors in your autumn scenic painting? Cover the walls with a tree-like design—green leaves and bark brown stems growing upward on a white background; this will give height to your foyer. On your floor, lay a shag rug with a sage green field and a pumpkin orange border. On your table place a dried flower arrangement in colors of pumpkin, sage green, goldenrod yellow and a dash of chrysanthemum pink. On either side of your mirror, I suggest brass sconces with clear glass hurricane chimneys.

Question: *I have a dreary upstairs hallway—no windows, five doors (two of which are always closed since they are closets) and one ceiling light fixture. The walls are mint green stucco; the carpeting is dark green. I want to retain the carpeting. I am wondering if it would be advisable to paint the walls, doors and woodwork all one color—a medium shade of green. There is no furniture in the hall because there is no room.*

Paint the doors opening into a hallway a different color than the wall.

You are so right; your hall does need a lift. Since your walls are stucco, you can't wallpaper. Why not paint your walls a cheery red or sunshine yellow? Paint all the trim, doors and ceiling a spanking white. From that one ceiling light fixture, hang a big, globular Japanese paper lamp in solid white. These airy, lovely lanterns shed lots of light. Though there's no room for furniture, I am sure there is room for a couple of plants. Why not put a Boston fern or two on plexiglass pedestals?

164

The Foyer and Hall

Question: *My new modern house has a foyer with a large window and a charcoal gray and black slate floor. The walls and doors are white. What colors do you suggest for a new throw rug and curtains? I have room for a table or bench in front of the window.*

Orange and yellow, plus black, gray and white, equals a modern foyer.

Find a throw rug that looks like a sunburst in mandarin orange and sunshine yellow swirls. You can have a table *and* benches by using a white lacquered Parsons table. Under the table, place two stainless steel X-frame benches topped with brilliant yellow vinyl. At the window, sheer open-weave casement curtains would allow a maximum amount of light into your foyer. You might accessorize your Parsons table with a guest book and a walnut stair baluster converted into a candle holder.

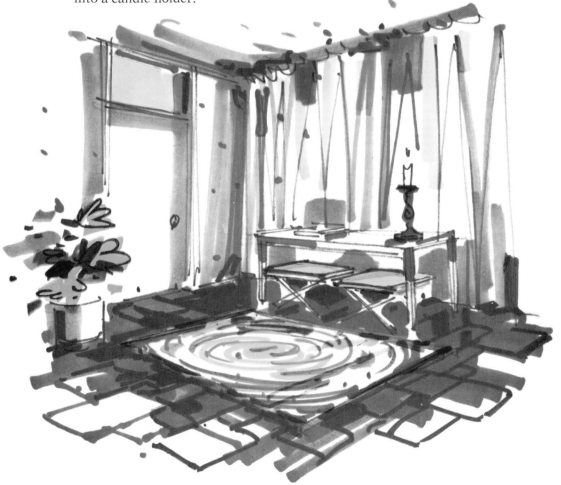

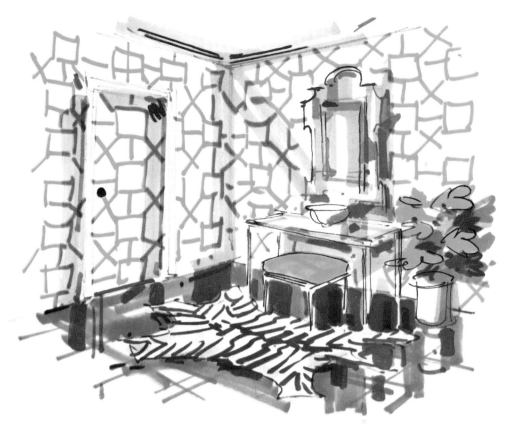

Question: *I am at a loss as to what to put on the walls of our small, dark foyer to make it seem bigger and brighter. There is room in the area for a table, and we have two we could put there—one a console table with a glass top on a stainless steel base, the other a heavy oak library table. The floor is brown vinyl. Can you help me decorate this room?*

Green and white trellis design wall covering opens up a small foyer.

Hang trellis design washable vinyl in emerald green on white on the walls. Cover the flat surface of all doors facing the foyer with the wall covering, too. This paper will lighten your foyer considerably and also enlarge it. The modern glass-top console table would be my choice, because it carries through the open look decorating philosophy. Place one of your prettiest bowls on the glass top for incoming mail. Over the console, hang a traditional Venetian mirror. A black and white zebra rug would be the delightful, unexpected note underfoot. A traditional white French bench with fluted legs, covered with melon velvet, would be a great accent color piece.

166

The Foyer and Hall

Question: *We have an entrance hall that I feel could use some color. I would like to wallpaper this area and wonder if you would suggest a color scheme. The floor is beige and rust quarry tile; woodwork is oak; walls are now off-white. In our adjoining living room there are parquet floors and medium blue shag area rugs. I've considered blue flock wallpaper to match these area rugs. Any suggestions?*

Warm up the coldness of tile floors in a foyer with multicolor wallpaper.

I think the blue flock wallpaper to match the blue shag area rugs would be a little dull. Why not select a happy yellow, light blue, royal-blue and cantaloupe geometric or stripe wall paper? These colors would look well with the rugs. Or try a trellis design on your hallway walls in a light blue or happy yellow on a white background. Trellis designs always open up space visually. With either wallpaper, paint your ceiling spanking white, and if you have room, I'd like to see a white wrought-iron chair or love seat with yellow and blue pillows.

Question: *We have a long hallway on the second floor of our home. All the bedrooms are off the hallway, and there is one window at the end of the hall that provides light. Can you suggest anything we can do to make the hall seem shorter and wider?*

Vinyl tiles laid horizontally in alternating stripes of color can shorten and widen a hall.

Why not lay horizontal stripes on your hallway floor, perhaps vinyl tile. Lay first a row of black vinyl tiles (9-inch or 12-inch squares); then a row of white vinyl tiles in the same dimension. The horizontal stripes will give the hall the illusion of being wider than it is. On the window at the end of your hall hang a louvered shutter of a brilliant color, maybe royal blue, aster pink or mustard. The bright color will attract the eye, and the far wall will not appear so far away. Also, anything you can hang on the hallway walls, such as prints or an arrangement or two of dried flowers, will help reduce the feeling of a long, cold tunnel.

Question: *We are going to carpet our upstairs hallway. Because it receives so much traffic, I want a dark and practical color. What the color is doesn't matter very much, since the bedrooms opening off the hall have only area rugs in several different colors. Also, I would like to paint the walls and ceiling of the hall. What colors do you suggest?*

Plum purple is a practical, popular color for a hallway carpet.

Choose a practical plum purple for your hall carpeting. Walls might be a sunshine yellow with bright white semigloss enamel for the trim, or they might be a mauve pink with pale melon orange flat paint for the trim. In either case, paint your ceiling white.

Question: *I really need your help on my problem entrance hall. There is virtually no wall space, as most of the space is taken up with doors and doorways. There is a brown and beige vinyl tile on the floor. On the wall I hung a long, dark mahogany clock, beneath which is a small, triangular, dark mahogany table with ornate legs. The living room, which is seen from the hall, is decorated in gold, olive green and off-white. Since the hall is terribly dark, what do you think of having a new front door installed with the top half of glass, or putting glass bricks around the door? Can you suggest a ceiling light? Would you wallpaper the hall and if so, in what?*

A foyer with little wall space should be painted a solid color.

Your entry hall has very little wall space, so I would stick with paint, perhaps a warm and friendly sunshine yellow. You might consider installing a new front door with the top half of glass, but I say "no" to glass bricks. Your brown and beige floor isn't helping the light problem. Why not consider installing white marbleized vinyl with a lemon yellow trellis design feature stripping? The feature stripping can be two inches wide, used with and separating white marbleized vinyl squares of a 12-inch square size. A vase of colorful fresh or dried flowers on your table will add brightness to the room. Select a handsome light fixture—one that coordinates with your setting. I would suggest a shiny brass fixture with white translucent shades. The shades might be trimmed in green velvet or in yellow or in melon.

168

The Foyer and Hall

Question: *Our entry foyer is paneled with walnut, and the floor is walnut-stain planks. The room is beginning to look like the country style I want. What shall I do for color and more "countryness"?*

Walnut beams can bring lots of country charm to a foyer.

For more country charm, install walnut-stained beams on the ceiling. For color, what about using an orange, yellow and burnt umber braided rug on the floor? A deacon's bench would be an attractive addition to the furnishings, especially with its seat covered in a jonquil yellow vinyl. For further colonial warmth and for keeping everyone on time, what about a grandfather's clock?

Question: *We have a long narrow hall with the bedroom doors all on one wall. The doors are plain flush doors. How can I make the hall look wider and more interesting?*

Use sheet mirror on the wall to widen a narrow hall.

Install sheet mirror on the wall opposite the doors, and create a dado on other walls and put moldings on the doors. Paint the chair rail, door frames and door moldings white semigloss enamel. The door surfaces can be painted royal blue lacquer. To complete the patriotic look, cover the walls above and below the chair rail with a bright red felt or vinyl. Give further width to your long hallway by installing stripes of blue and white vinyl tiles 24-inches wide on the floor. You could also install the same widths of carpet using inexpensive carpet samples.

170

The Foyer and Hall

Question: *Both the living room and kitchen open into our L-shaped entrance foyer. The living room colors are off-white and lime green; the kitchen is pink. There is beige carpeting in the living room and the foyer. What color should we put on the foyer walls?*

Paper a foyer in stripes of colors picked up from adjacent rooms.

I think your foyer walls would look great in a striped pattern wallpaper of lime green, shocking pink, white and beige.

Question: *Our current decorating problem is the foyer and bedroom hallway of our one story ranch house. As you enter the foyer the family room and kitchen are to the right; straight ahead is the living/dining room; to the left is a very long, windowless hall with four bedrooms opening off it. The living room is the room most visible from the foyer. It has white walls, draperies in a floral pattern of orange, melon, pink, blue and green, two sofas in the same floral pattern, a chair in light blue velvet. The carpeting in the living room, the foyer and hall is gold. What do we do with the walls in the foyer and hall—paint or paper them? What furnishing should we consider?*

Make a foyer and connecting hall a definite room of the house with strikingly colorful wallpaper.

There should be some harmony of color between your living room and the foyer and hallway. I wouldn't paint this area, however. I think you should consider this a real room. Begin by selecting a formal looking fabric with melon, avocado and gold stripes. Have the fabric paperbacked, and hang it just like wallpaper. Woodwork should be white semigloss enamel. In the foyer I'd put a Parsons table painted a bright avocado green lacquer. The table would be a good place to display an attractive piece of sculpture. If there is room, you might find one of those wonderful brass umbrella stands and put that in the foyer, too. For the hall, I'd recommend a grouping of black and white prints in narrow gold frames—great fun for your family to collect.

Question: *My house has a fairly large entry with a lovely curved stairway and white walls. It should be exciting and dramatic, but it just seems big and dull. What color scheme would solve my problem?*

A black and white parquet type floor is both practical and dramatic in a foyer, especially if there is a curving stairway carpeted in a brilliant third color.

Install black and white 12-inch square vinyl tiles on the floor of your foyer to achieve a parquet effect. Select a brilliant color, such as emerald green, for stair carpeting. In the curve of your staircase, put a small round table and drape it with a blue green cloth. Surround the table with four sitting stools covered in emerald green. You can use the table for an overflow dinner crowd or card playing parties. Keep a big vase of fresh or dried flowers on the table.

172

The Foyer and Hall

Question: *The rather large foyer of my apartment has a flagstone patterned vinyl floor. The walls are white, including several white painted metal folding closet doors. One wall area is an unframed mirror. The result is a cold, barren, blah look. Can you suggest something to bring a little warmth into this area? The adjoining living room is gold, moss green and black.*

If you use mirrors in your foyer, make certain they reflect beautiful colors.

Your foyer indeed sounds dull and cold and flat. Why don't you paint the doors a rich red-orange with white trim? Lay an interesting area rug on your foyer floor, maybe a melon and gold bamboo design on a white background.